SHORT • SCENIC • WALKS

SOUTH PENNINES

PAUL H

CW01661579

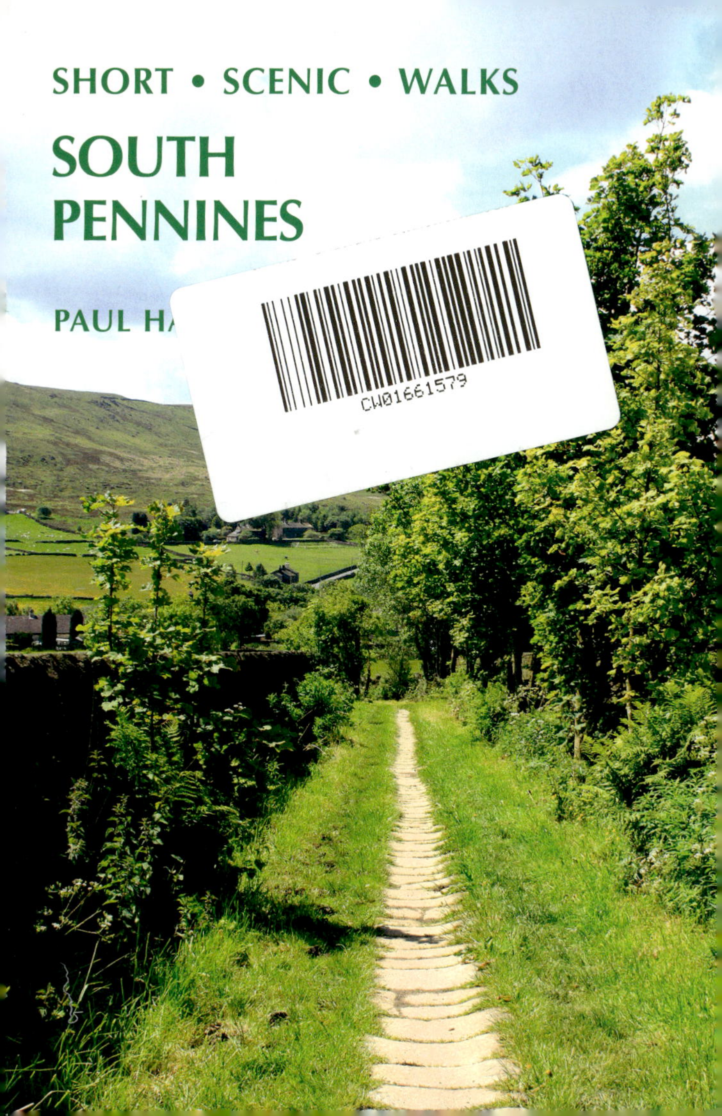

HILLSIDE PUBLICATIONS
38 Westburn Avenue, Keighley, West Yorkshire BD22 6AW

First Published 2023 © Paul Hannon 2023

ISBN 978 1 907626 42 5

While the author has walked and researched all these routes for the purposes of this guide, no responsibility can be accepted for any unforeseen circumstances encountered whilst following them

Sketch maps based on OS 1947 1-inch maps

Cover illustrations: Bilberry Reservoir; Hebden Bridge
Back cover: Pots & Pans, Saddleworth; Page 1: At Lumbutts
(Paul Hannon/Yorkshire Photo Library)

Printed in China on behalf of Latitude Press

HILLSIDE GUIDES... cover much of Northern England

•50 Yorkshire Walks For All •Journey of the Wharfe (photobook)

Short Scenic Walks •Teesdale & Weardale •Ribble Valley & Bowland •Wharfedale & Ilkley •Three Peaks & Malham •Arnside & Lunesdale •North York Moors •Harrogate & Nidderdale •South Pennines •Wensleydale •Haworth & Aire Valley •Ambleside & South Lakeland •Pendle & Lancashire Moors •Swaledale •Sedbergh & Dentdale

Walking in Yorkshire
•Aire Valley & Bronte Country
•Nidderdale & Ripon
•Wharfedale & Malham
•North York Moors South & West
•Yorkshire Wolds
•South Yorkshire
•Richmondshire & Hambleton
•Calderdale & South Pennines
•Three Peaks & Howgill Fells
•Wensleydale & Swaledale
•North York Moors North & East
•Harrogate & Ilkley
•West Yorkshire Countryside
•Howardian Hills & Vale of York

Lancashire/Cumbria •Pendle & the Ribble •Eden Valley

Long Distance •Dales Way •Coast to Coast Walk •Pendle Way

Visit us at www.hillsidepublications.co.uk

Ashway Cross, Dove Stone

Stoodley Pike

CONTENTS

INTRODUCTION

The South Pennines form a northerly continuation of the Peak District, based around the Calder, Colne, Holme and Tame Valleys. Calderdale is focused on Hebden Bridge and Todmorden, while the Holme Valley is based on Holmfirth, the Colne Valley on Marsden, and the Tame Valley on Uppermill. While Saddleworth and Littleborough sit on the western side of the Pennines, the former is a little corner of Yorkshire claimed by Lancashire since 1974.

Highlights of this fascinating region include landmark towers on Stoodley Pike, Castle Hill and Pots & Pans, the National Trust's Marsden Moor, the wonders of Standedge Tunnel, the rocky edges of Dove Stone and the rich woodland of Hardcastle Crags. The area oozes character shaped in part by the Industrial Revolution. You're never far from its evidence, be it canals, reservoirs, quarries, turnpike roads or packhorse trails. The hillsides are laced with a network of these old trade routes, and many stone causeways have survived. Hugging the valley bottoms are the Rochdale and the Huddersfield Narrow Canals. Tumbling to the floor of the upper dales are deep-cut, richly wooded little valleys known as cloughs, while up on the tops one is never far from a reservoir. This is grit-stone country, and sharing the higher ground are gnarled outcrops such as the Bride Stones, Raven Stones and Blackstone Edge.

The majority of walks are on rights of way or established access areas and paths: a handful which cross Open Access land are noted as such. Most days of the year you can freely walk here, but dogs are banned from grouse moors other than on rights of way. These areas can occasionally be closed, most likely from the grouse-shooting season's August start, though weekends should largely be unaffected: details from Natural England and information centres. Whilst the route description should be sufficient to guide you around, a map is recommended for greater information and interest: Ordnance Survey Explorer map OL21 covers 21 of the walks, with others served by maps OL1 and 288.

Information/Visitor Centres

- 15 Burnley Road **Todmorden** OL14 7BU (01706-818181)
- The Library **Holmfirth** HD9 3JH (01484-414868)
- Standedge Tunnel **Marsden** HD7 6NQ (01484-242792)
- **Hollingworth Lake** OL15 0AQ (01706-373421)
- Saddleworth Museum **Uppermill** OL3 6HS (01457-870336)

SOUTH PENNINES

30 Short Scenic Walks

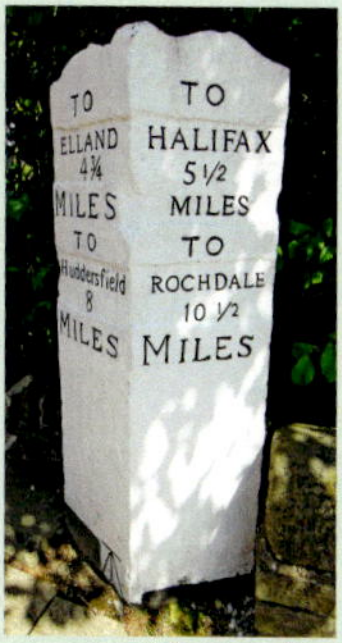

Ripponden

1 DIGGLE

4¾ miles from Uppermill

A steady ramble through fields with a colourful towpath return

Start *Village centre (SD 996057; OL3 6AP), car parks*
Map *OS Explorer OL1, Peak District, Dark Peak*

Uppermill is the principal settlement of Saddleworth, a collection of hugely characterful villages around the headwaters of the River Tame. Leave High Street by Church Road alongside a Methodist church. Merging with New Street, keep on the short way past a millpond to a former rail bridge, after which turn up steps on the left and head away on the old line. Becoming a broad track past sports fields into open country, it rises to an access road. Turn right on a cart track to a kissing-gate just ahead, sending an enclosed fieldside track with views to the moorland backdrop of Pots & Pans above Saddleworth church. In the next field, ignore a branch right and keep on the top edge to a stile at the end. The briefly fenced path drops right, then on with an old fence to a footbridge in a wooded clough. Climbing away up the other side, the path becomes enclosed then forks. Either will lead up to a back road by Saddleworth church, the left being nicer. Turn right to St Chad's with its stocks of 1698, and the Church Inn alongside.

Turn up an enclosed path by the front of the church, through a bridle-gate into Ivy Bank Farm. Rising past the buildings, as the drive swings right, instead take a stile left. An enclosed path heads away to cross a tiny clough, and from a stile go faintly on a sloping field beneath Wickens Farm. Across another small clough, go straight on above a deep, dry groove on the left. At the top bear right to a kissing-gate onto a road at Running Hill Head. Almost opposite, a snicket squeezes between gardens at this hamlet, emerging into a field. Enclosed as far as a stile, cross a track to a gateway. Through it, leave the track and follow the right-hand wall down to a corner gate/stile. Resume on the other side of the wall, and at the bottom the head of a green way is met. Turn left on this, through a gate at the end and along a fieldside to a gate/stile at Back o' th' Lee.

After the houses, leave the drive after a cattle-grid and turn right to join a crumbling, descending wall. Through an old wall at the bottom, drop steadily left to bridge a channel onto a path at the bottom. This runs pleasantly to the left alongside the drain, over intervening stiles and at the end dropping onto a narrow road. Go right into Diggle, rising right at a fork to the Diggle Hotel. At the junction beneath the pub take the road over the railway, with the tunnel entrance on the right. At the bridge end go briefly left, and at the next bend turn left into a car park. At the end you join the Huddersfield Narrow Canal at Standedge Tunnel's southern portal.

The return route is infallible as you follow the canal back to Uppermill, with several refreshment opportunities. With paths on either bank, you will later be forced onto the left bank. En route, the Diggle Flight of locks leads down to the A670 bridge under which is Wool Road transhipment warehouse, where goods were loaded on and off narrowboats. The route resumes under the A6052 bridge past Brownhill countryside centre, after which you bridge the River Tame beneath Saddleworth Viaduct. The last stage leads uneventfully back into Uppermill, where you are forced up onto Moorgate Street to finish.

Standedge Tunnel re-opening at Diggle, 2001

2 POTS & PANS

4¼ miles from Greenfield

A superb walk on grand paths to a fine little hill

Start *Binn Green (SE 017044; OL3 7NN), 1½ miles east on A635: RSPB car park and lay-by*
Map *OS Explorer OL1, Peak District, Dark Peak*

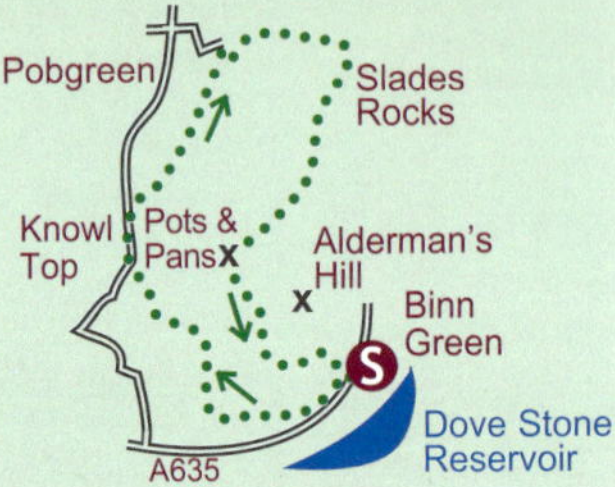

Return to the road and cross to the broad, rough track of Long Lane heading left. Over a brow it runs a lengthy, level walled course beneath Alderman's Hill, with Dove Stone Reservoir to your left: on rounding a corner, Pots & Pans monument appears on the skyline above. Keep straight on at a cross-paths, improving into a superb old footway. Across a tiny clough, briefly escape a reedy tract to resume a nice rise to a brow. A fence leads on to a gate onto a firmer track from the left, and on the short way further to a road at Knowl Top Farm. Advance along, and at Knowl Farm drive on the left, take an unsigned, flagged drive rising right to approach a lone house, Spring Head. Don't follow it down but take a stile in front, and a faint path runs on above the garden. A gurgling spring is passed and the little path runs an excellent level course. Traversing the slopes through several pastures with stiles, a brief spell of heather moorland is also enjoyed. Your way ultimately becomes enclosed to enter the old weaving hamlet of Pobgreen.

The access road is joined beneath impressive three-storeyed Lamb Lodge. Instead turn right up the continuation of the access road, rapidly losing its surface and transforming into a grassy, walled way. Meeting a cart track at the top, follow it through the gate above and resume on its fading wallside course. Higher, where the track bears left, continue up steeper slopes where sunken pathways climb to the edge of the moorland plateau. By now there are panoramic views back over Saddleworth.

Through an old wall at the top, the path turns right along the moor edge between fence and old wall above the tumble of Slades

Rocks. As the wall drops away, the path advances with the fence to a corner, where across a stile it rises briefly to the tilted outcrops of Shaw Rocks. Here fork right, slanting across to quickly meet a broader path: slant down this to a minor dip before a short rise through a fence-stile and old wall to find the war memorial on Pots & Pans just below. To the right before it are the shapely Kinder Stones. The sturdy monument was erected by Saddleworth folk in honour of their Great War dead. Alderman's Hill brings this spur of moorland to a shapely culmination over to the left.

Leave by a grassy path heading south the few yards to the Pots & Pan Stone. Beneath it the path slants left, down past an old quarry to an old wall corner. Continue down with a fence to a path crossroads by a wall at Edge End. Turn left over a fence-stile to rise gently away with the old wall-cum-fence. Swinging right, ignore a broader branch rising left, and remain with the wall on a thin trod which maintains this course to curve around beneath Alderman's Hill. Splendid rockscapes just above vie for attention with the prospect across to the Dove Stone edges above the reservoir. When the wall turns sharply away, you meet an ascending path: turn right on it down the wallside, passing new tree plantings. Towards the bottom, ideally take a branch left to slant down to a stile back onto the start of Long Lane.

Pots & Pans

3 RAVEN STONES

$4\frac{1}{4}$ miles from Greenfield

Spectacular rock scenery and archetypal moorland paths

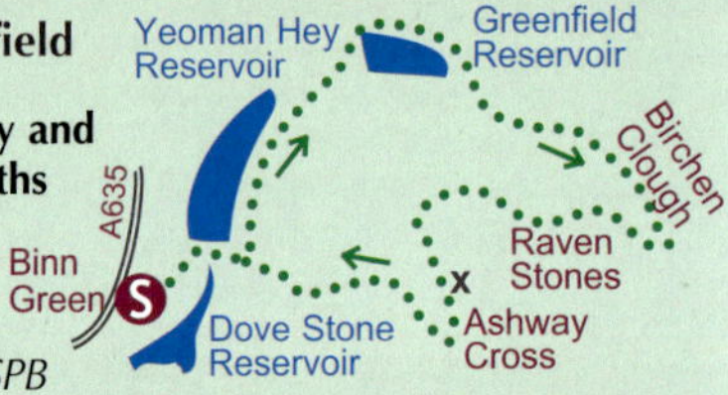

***Start** Binn Green (SE 017044; OL3 7NN), $1\frac{1}{2}$ miles east on A635: RSPB car park and lay-by **Map** OS Explorer OL1, Peak District, Dark Peak **Access** Open Access, see page 4. The route demands a little agility on a very short but straightforward climb on rock*

From the car park beneath the prow of Alderman's Hill, drop down a broad path into trees, then briefly more steeply to a stile onto a surfaced access road. Go left, through a gate beneath Binn Green houses, to arrive at the dam of Yeoman Hey Reservoir beneath Ashway Rocks. Cross the dam, with Dove Stone Reservoir below, and take a path branching left. This runs on above the lake with a fence to your right. A wall takes over and the path runs to a broad bridge beneath Greenfield Reservoir's grassy dam. Don't cross, but take a path bearing right to run above a drain to a small footbridge across it. Go left on the dam foot and up the grassy embankment by the outflow, bridging it at the top to join an access road. Turn right to run the length of this smaller lake, continuing as a stony track rising gently with Greenfield Brook to end in front of a lagoon beneath two bouldery ravines. A small gate accesses a drain footbridge into the foot of the right-hand Birchen Clough.

The main path crosses the stream within 100 yards to squeeze between a pair of boulders beneath an old wall, then commences a sometimes bouldery ascent near the stream. Reaching a massive boulder with another perched on it, advance just yards further to a fork. Here bear right on the path towards the stream to approach a super waterfall. Here you undertake a modest scramble of a few feet of sturdy rock up to your left. Above the waterfall resume past a deep pool: the going soon eases, and though still bouldery it runs a super course, at times on streamside slabs. Now virtually level on the open moor, the intermittently peaty path quickly runs to an obvious crossing point, a good place to unwind.

Across the stream a broad path rises directly away before turning right to contour along, absorbing a direct slanting path. A distinct edge forms to guide your imperceptibly rising path along to the Raven Stones, whose major feature is the inspiring pinnacle suitably named the Trinnacle. Resume on the edge path, a classic stride above outcrops looking down on the reservoir. As the rocks abate, the main path bears left away from the edge, contouring beneath gentle slopes above the shelf of Little Flat. Before reaching Ashway Rocks ahead, a cross-path is met, with another just beyond. Turn left here to climb to a higher plateau, by now looking down on Dove Stone Reservoir. The grand path heads away to quickly arrive at Ashway Cross, a memorial to James Platt, MP for Oldham, the victim of a shooting accident during a grouse shoot in 1857.

The path continues on a very gentle drop to the solitary Ashway Stone, where a little path drops a very short way onto another level path. Ignoring that dropping away, turn right on this to contour on before dropping gently towards Ashway Rocks. It drops left before them and along to a fork, where the right branch crosses the short way onto a path dropping from the boulders: Yeoman Hey Reservoir returns to view, with the dark wall of Dove Stone Rocks across to your left. Turn left, dropping through bracken to a stile in a fence, then broadly and directly down onto a firm, level path. Go right a few yards to rejoin the outward route, re-crossing Yeoman Hey's dam to finish as you began.

Dove Stone Rocks across Dove Stone Reservoir

4 HOLMBRIDGE LAKELAND

4 miles from Digley

Attractive reservoirs in the folds of Black Hill

Start *Digley Reservoir (SE 110072; HD9 2QD), Yorkshire Water car park on north side*
Map *OS Explorer OL21, South Pennines* ***or*** *Explorer 288, Bradford & Huddersfield*

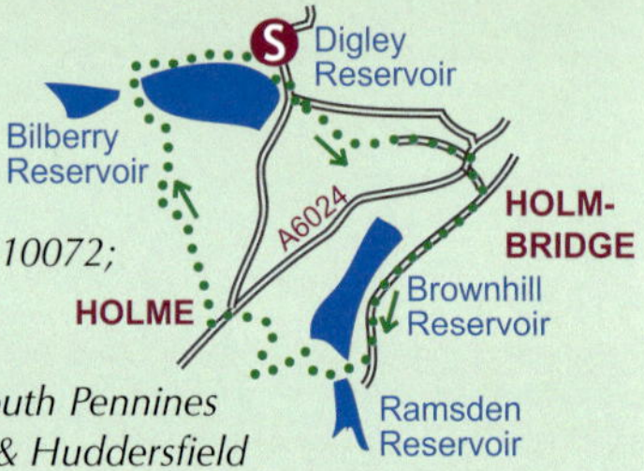

From a gateway on the reservoir side of the entrance, cross a broad path to a gap sending a path down a heathery bank above the reservoir to rejoin the road. With big views over the water to Black Hill, continue the short way to a road junction at the dam end. Don't cross, but continue down the road to a kissing-gate on the right. A path briefly parallels the road before slanting through a small wood, and from a corner kissing-gate descends steps onto Digley Road. Turn left for a traffic-free descent to Holmbridge above Digley Brook, the surface improving before emerging onto the A6024. The village features St David's church and the Bridge pub.

Turn right over the bridge, then left on a side road signed to Ramsden Reservoir. When it splits, take the right branch climbing to a junction. Keep straight on past several houses to the dam of Brownhill Reservoir, and on to approach a lay-by just short of Ramsden Reservoir. Just short of the dam a track turns down towards it, and an enclosed path crosses just below its crest. At the end it slants away from the dam: ignoring an early branch left, rise through trees onto a knoll on the spur between Brownhill Reservoir's two arms. It then runs above the bank of Netherley Wood until dropping to a footbridge above a lovely waterfall on Rake Dike.

Slanting back up the other side, the path levels out to leave the trees at a stile, then up a rough pasture to adjacent stiles at the corner above a wood. An enclosed path rises to two small gates: from the left one continue up a fieldside to a gate. The broader enclosed way runs out to the A6024 on the edge of Holme. Turn left as far as a cobbled square, passing castellated Holme Castle and a former school of 1838. Just within the Peak District National Park boundary, Holme boasts attractive cottages including three-storeyed weavers' houses, and the Fleece Inn and a WC.

Turn right up through the square and along cul-de-sac Meal Hill Road. As it bends left to rise to a school, turn right through a gate and along a grassy walled way. At the end cross the field to a stile at the foot of the opposite wall, then continue above a wall, with Digley Reservoir appearing. The waymarked path crosses a string of pastures linked by assorted stiles, occasionally slanting right as the reservoir increasingly features. At the end the path drops right onto a broader path. Turn left through a bridle-gate, and rising away, it takes another in the adjacent wall into colourful terrain near the reservoir. The path drops to its head, which is also Bilberry Reservoir's embankment. This charming spot was the scene of an 1852 damburst, causing 81 fatalities as a torrent raced down the valley to Holmfirth. Across it a track slants away, doubling back right up to a junction on open ground. Turning right, this runs on to become a path fringing trees enclosing Digley Reservoir. It quickly rejoins a track at the point where the old sunken way runs forlornly into the waters. This rises past an old quarry and on to the car park.

Digley Reservoir

5 HOLME VALLEY

4 miles from Holmfirth

Exploring old hamlets and an unsung riverbank

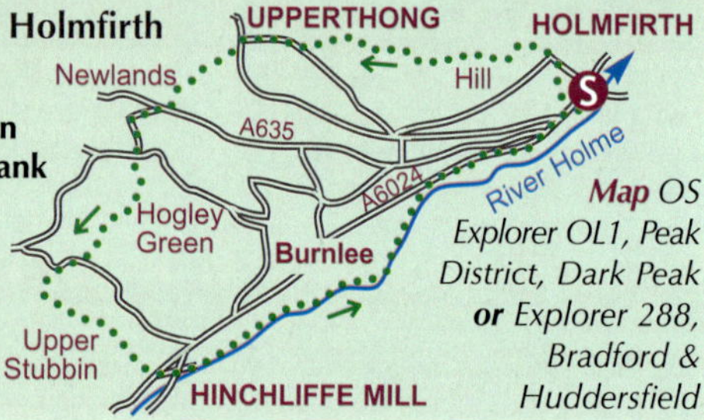

Start *Town centre (SE 141081; HD9 1HA), car parks*

Map *OS Explorer OL1, Peak District, Dark Peak* **or** *Explorer 288, Bradford & Huddersfield*

Holmfirth is a characterful place of nooks and crannies, famed for Bamforth's saucy seaside postcards and TV's 'Last of the Summer Wine'. From the junction of Victoria Street with the main road, go left a few strides on Huddersfield Road, and just before the Library/Information Centre, take a path climbing right into Victoria Park. Remain on the main setted path which curves up to the right, crossing a broad, level path. From the top corner a snicket runs out onto a road, Cooper Lane. Turn up this to a T-junction with Binns Lane just ahead. Go right a few yards and turn up a path between gardens. This climbs steeply through trees to run out between drives onto an access road at Hill. Go left on the walled track of Hill Lane, running unfailingly on to rise to meet a road bend at Upperthong.

Head straight along Towngate, passing the Royal Oak pub to a junction with Wickens Lane at the end. Bear left down Broad Lane through a sharp bend out of the village, and within yards take a stile on the right. Cross the field centre to the next, then turn down the wallside to a stile onto a rough lane. Go right, down past the house at Newlands onto the A635. Cross to descend Black Sike Lane into Hart Holes Clough, and up the other side to a junction, where turn right. Immediately beyond, as the road opens out at Hogley Green, turn left on a driveway, and keep left at a fork to pass between houses to the old hamlet of Hogley. Swing right between the buildings to a gate/stile into a field. Head away with the wall, crossing to the other side at a corner stile. From the next stile drop across the field centre to one opposite, then advance with a wall down to a stile onto Cold Well Lane.

Go right just as far as a lone house, a former Sunday School of 1816. An enclosed path turns down its far side, swinging down to a kissing-gate before a sharp bend at a junction. Ignore the corner stile and turn left down this broad, enclosed way, dropping gently to a gate/stile at the head of Stubbin Clough. The path runs a splendid grassy route above the clough edge, and down to join a drive. Don't follow it down through the houses, but cross straight over, quickly turning left through a gap between houses at Upper Stubbin. Through a gate into a field, a largely stone path descends to a gate at the bottom, where Stubbin Lane drops to the A6024 at Hinchliffe Mill. To the left are a shop and the Stumble Inn.

Cross straight over and bear left on Old Road to an angled crossroads with Ford Gate, and at the end go straight ahead on Water Street past old millworkers' cottages. Into the mill yard keep straight on past the mill to a footbridge on the River Holme. Don't cross, but head downstream on a path between mill-race and river. This runs through wooded surrounds to a large millpond backed by Bottoms Mill at Burnlee. Towards the end drop to a river bridge, and without crossing, resume downstream on a path between mill and river. Beyond the mill the path runs past a weir to new housing, where a cobbled section leads up to the A6024. Turn right on the footway back into town.

Weavers House, Upperthong

6 Castle Hill

4¼ miles from Farnley Tyas

Engaging woodland around an iconic hilltop landmark

Start *Village centre (SE 164127; HD4 6UD), roadside parking*
Map *OS Explorer 288, Bradford & Huddersfield*

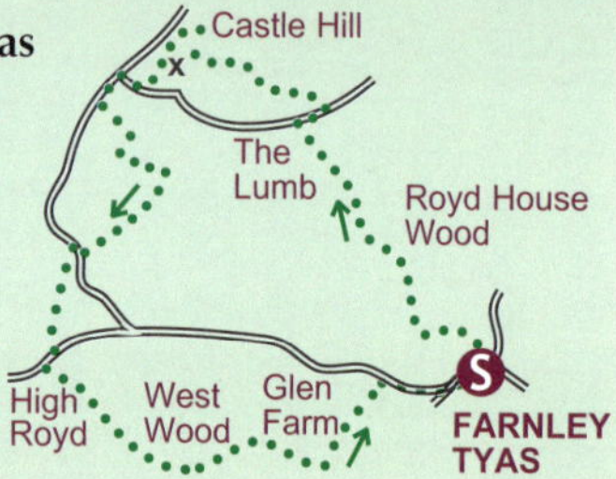

Facing the Golden Cock pub go right a few strides then left at the junction, then rapidly left down an enclosed cart track. Bending left to end at a bench, through a kissing-gate turn down the field-side to a gate/stile part-way down. A broad path descends Royd House Wood, crossing a streamlet and on to briefly emerge. Quickly re-entering trees, it runs briefly level to leave trees at the other side. Pass right of the wall heading away, a path shadowing its continuing hedge down to a stile at the end. A path heads away through Molly Carr Wood, descending steps to Lumb Dike. A bridge crosses the stream, and the path ascends to a gate. Ascend the field with a fence on your left, and up a second one to a stile at The Lumb.

Turn briefly right on Lumb Lane to a stile on the left, for a steep fieldside climb to a stile. Resume uphill to a stile onto an access road. A stile to your left maintains the climb, becoming enclosed in greenery to slant left into undergrowth. At the rear of a house, a path doubles back right to emerge at a fence with open views. Just above is the outer bank of Castle Hill fort. Follow the path right with the fence onto the end of the site, where rise to meet a firm path encircling the outer bank. Go right on this round the fort's other side to the Victoria Tower commemorating the monarch's Diamond Jubilee of 1897. Normally open holiday and weekend afternoons, for a fee you can climb to survey the far-reaching panorama. The hill is best known for its Iron Age hillfort, whose distinctive ramparts and ditches were incorporated into the defences of a castle 800 years ago.

Leave by a hard path running a few strides from the tower to steps down to a road. Go right to a junction, then left. At the second house on the left take a stile set back across its yard, and follow a wall away. At a kink turn right across the field centre to an outer corner, and through a gateway turn left to resume along the wall. Through an intervening stile, this leads to a gateway in the bottom wall. Through it turn sharp right to a gate/stile above Roaf Wood, and on again through a corner stile ahead. Leaving the wood edge, rise with a wall on your left. At a bend part-way up, pass through a stile, and a thin path turns right with the wall onto Hey Lane.

Cross and go right a few strides to a gate/stile, and take the path heading away with a hedge on the right. Dropping to a fence-stile, take the left fork down to a stile into Upper Park Wood. Drop left down the edge to a gate to run a level course onto Honley Road at High Royd. Cross and go briefly right, then take an access road left. Leave by a path right above the final house, into a field, then descend the centre into trees. Ignoring an early fork right, drop to cross a stream. Up the bank into open pasture, the path rises into West Wood. Take the main path rising to a cart track, crossing it to slant left to the top. Go left to emerge above a scrubby bank, soon reaching a fork: keep left along the bank top. Towards the end is an old stile into wooded Sawgates Clough, a good path tracing the wood top to cross the streamlet. The path then ascends steps to a gap into a field corner. Rise away with an old wall on your left, soon easing. Maintain this course past Glen Farm, and on to a stile onto Honley Road. Cross to a footway and rise the short way back.

Castle Hill

7 ROYD EDGE CLOUGH

4 miles from Meltham

Good paths and tracks from a delightful catchwater to moorland and a colourful side valley

Start *Town centre (SE 099106; HD9 4AE), car parks*
Map *OS Explorer 288, Bradford & Huddersfield*

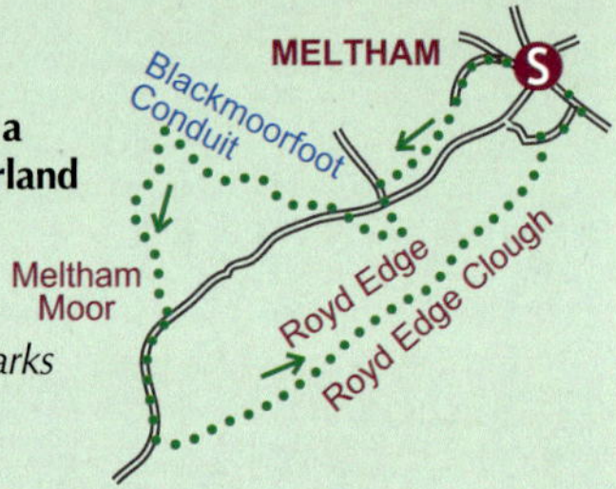

Meltham is a strongly independent cross between large village and small town, with streets featuring shops, pubs and cafes radiating from near St Bartholomew's church. A short branch line from the Huddersfield-Sheffield railway opened in 1868 and fully closed in 1965, while until 1988 Meltham was renowned for the production of David Brown tractors. From the central junction, cross the main road and head along Greens End Road left of the church. Curving round behind it, go left up suburban Colders Lane. At the top it narrows at some older houses, and transforms into an inviting, narrow path. Rising very pleasantly between walls it emerges onto a road, Leygards Lane.

Go left to a crossroads with Wessenden Head Road, and straight over to ascend a rough access road. Alongside Upper Calders Farm take a wall-stile on the right, sending a permissive path away along the old catchwater drain of Blackmoorfoot Conduit. Beyond a bridge crossing, it runs on to the road again beneath a lone house. Across, resume as before but now for a much longer spell. Fine views look to Meltham Moor up above, while to your right back over town are the landmarks of Meltham Cop, Castle Hill and Emley Moor TV mast. After crossing three further farmers' access bridges, you finally arrive at a gate/stile onto the head of a track, Brow Grains Road.

Go left to a gate onto the open moor, and leave the rising track in favour of one through a gate on your left. As High Moor Edge Road this rises away with a wall along the foot of the moor.

Continually rising, you pass above a wood and up further to ultimately meet an access road from isolated West Nab Cottage. This runs left the short way back onto Wessenden Head Road. Turn up it for a few minutes, over a cattle-grid with the open moor above displaying a fine bouldery crest. Soon reaching the end of the adjacent wall at the walk's high point, a fence-stile marks the start of your infallible return route.

A super green path descends the grassy moor alongside the dead-straight wall. Over to your right are the colourful upper reaches of Royd Edge Clough, while ahead, Meltham is foreground to a distant view eastwards out from the hills. Through a couple of kissing-gates, a heather tract is replaced by grass pasture to reach a stile/gate onto a rough access road on the valley edge. Continue along this with the clough now firmly alongside, and when it swings away left, simply continue down a still broad path. Towards the bottom it becomes surfaced by a graveyard. Just past a junction below, at Laithe Farm, a kissing-gate on the left sends a firm path alongside allotments to emerge onto a suburban road. Cross straight over to resume on a short-lived, surfaced course out onto the next street, Tinker Lane. Turn right to emerge onto the main road, and go left the couple of minutes back to the centre. Passed on your right is the Odd Fellows Hall of 1851.

Descending Royd Edge, with Castle Hill beyond

8 COLNE VALLEY

4¼ miles from Slaithwaite

Colourful cloughs and canal towpath

Start *Village centre (SE 079139; HD7 5AS), Old Bank car park*

Map *OS Explorer OL21, South Pennines*

From the mini-roundabout at Britannia Road and Station Road, turn left along Market Place, passing the Shoulder of Mutton pub and beneath the church of St James. Quickly bear left on Nabbs Lane, passing between the Manor House with its adjacent former lock-up, and the Silent Woman pub. The road bears right as Holme Lane, rising beneath a railway viaduct. A steep climb leads to a path right across the dam of Slaithwaite (Hill Top) Reservoir. Over the outflow bridge turn left on a path along the bank, by a mill-cut. This leads increasingly pleasantly to the wooded reservoir head. Passing a weir at the start of the mill-cut, lovely surroundings lead up to a small dam. While the right of way continues up the broad track onto a road then left the short way to Clough House Bridge, locals use the path over the smaller dam, then right to cross the outflow above a waterfall into a small ravine. The path then goes left to bridge the main stream for a short climb onto a wood-top path. This runs right above the clough edge to a kissing-gate onto a road.

Go right the short way down to Clough House Bridge, over which take a gate on the left and resume upstream into Merry Dale Clough. This splendid ramble ignores an early footbridge, a faint path staying close to the stream as it burbles through scrubby pastures. This continues for some time until reaching an impasse as a grassy bridge crosses the stream. Don't cross but take the path right, rising through a tiny cutting and past a pond on the left. A snicket and steps rise past the house at Merry Dale, up with a streamlet to join the drive for the final yards onto setted Tyas Lane.

Double back left down this narrow old packhorse route to a stone-arched bridge in Bradshaw Clough. It winds steeply up the other side as the narrow, variously surfaced bridleway of Scout Lane to emerge onto a drive. Go straight ahead and over a crossroads to the perfectly located Rose & Crown pub at Cop Hill.

Beyond it the narrow road drops away with super views, and within five minutes turn left down Green Lane. Steepening near the bottom, turn right on a cart track to an isolated house. Pass the front to adjacent stiles sending a delectable green way dropping down the heathery bank of Booth Naze, with Marsden ahead beneath high moors. Part enclosed, it narrows as it drops to a streamlet in Booth Gate Clough. Go left down its near side, soon becoming enclosed to a stile onto a road junction. Go straight ahead under the rail bridge, and at the bend below continue down the access road through the hamlet of Booth. Swinging left at the bottom to a lone house, a path advances a few yards further to bridge the Huddersfield Narrow Canal at a lovely corner with a holding basin and a lock. Turn left to follow the towpath back to the start. Features of interest include a number of descending locks (one of which is a vertical 'guillotine' lock), the occasional company of the River Colne, and a busy scene alongside Upper Mill, which includes a bakery/cafe. From here the tarmac finish is shared with vehicles.

Huddersfield Narrow Canal, Booth

9 Wessenden Valley

4½ miles from Marsden

Moorland and reservoirs in the Peak District's northernmost valley

Start *Church, Towngate (SE 047116; HD7 6DJ), roadside parking*
Map *OS Explorer OL1, Peak District, Dark Peak & Explorer OL21, South Pennines*
Access *Open Access (tiny section on National Trust land)*

From St Bartholomew's church, cross Towngate to a green with the grave of machine-maker and Luddite-enemy Enoch Taylor. Go straight ahead to a bridge and into the Market Place. Advance to the front of the Mechanics Hall, then turn right past shops up Peel Street. Across the A62 at the top, continue up alongside a park. At a T-junction with Carrs Road, go left a few yards then take a drive doubling back uphill. A stiff pull leads to its demise at the top, entering the yard of a house in front. Go left between stables and house to a gate in front of another house. Go sharp right between fences to steps sending a path up into open country. Rising as a sunken way towards moorland slopes, it quickly slants right. Soon levelling out, it now runs a super, largely enclosed way beneath colourful Binn Edge. Ahead is sprawling moorland, while down to your right is the massive Bank Bottom Mills beneath Pule Hill.

Advance through a small gate, and after a kissing-gate the way runs behind ruinous Binn House, then rises slightly to a gate into Peters Farm. Continue along the short drive out to a bend of Binn Lane. Go left, briefly uphill then on for a short half-mile, serving several houses before losing its surface after Binn Lodge Farm. Just a few yards further the track ends, with a fine Wessenden prospect including Blakeley Reservoir. Through a bridle-gate in front onto Binn Moor, two paths head away. The right one slants down through open country to a bridge in Rams Clough. Rise up the other side by a wall, soon easing out at a ruin on your left. Continue up with a reedy hollow between you and the wall. A little further, the path slants more determinedly left to rise to a stone-arched bridge on redundant Deer Hill Conduit.

Turn right on the embanked path to commence a lengthy stride in its company. Several old bridges are passed, and a stile crossed at the head of Great Clough. Big views look over Blakeley and Butterley reservoirs. After another stile the drain abruptly ends, but the path continues across moorland on Hey Brinks, entering bracken. Wessenden Reservoir soon appears below, and yards further a path branches right, in line with the dam, to descend steeply through bracken. At the bottom it runs a few strides right onto a wallside path, doubling back left to the Pennine Way path by the dam. Turn down a few yards to pass a bridge over the outflow, and down the rough road past Wessenden Lodge. You pass above the lengths of both Blakeley and the larger Butterley Reservoir, beyond whose dam you rejoin Binn Road. Leave at once by a mighty flight of sturdy steps beneath a heather bank, and at the bottom advance along an access road. Passing Bank Bottom Mills you emerge back onto Binn Road. Cross the mini-roundabout and along Fall Lane, quickly forking left under the A62 to emerge by the church.

Butterley Reservoir from Great Clough

10 MARSDEN MOOR

4¾ miles from Marsden

A wealth of interest from towpath to moorland

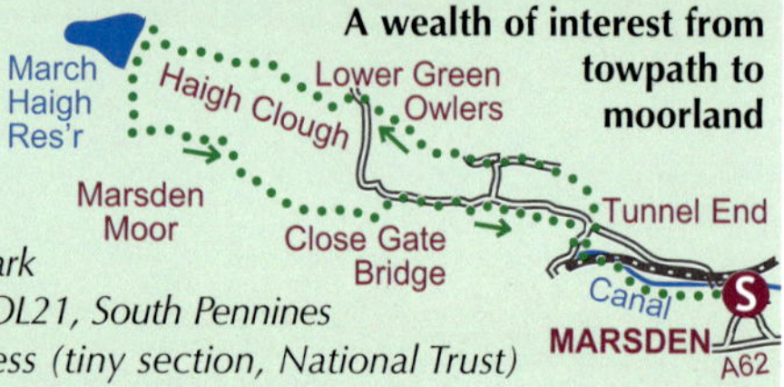

Start *Rail station (SE 046118; HD7 6DH), car park*
Map *OS Explorer OL21, South Pennines*
Access *Open Access (tiny section, National Trust)*

Facing the station, go left to join the Huddersfield Narrow Canal at a lock, then left on the towpath for ten minutes. Passing under low rail bridges you emerge opposite a visitor centre in an old warehouse at Tunnel End: just past it, rise to a bridge. The canal's focal point also features a cafe at Standedge Tunnel entrance, with boat trips. The canal was built to link canals at Huddersfield and Dukinfield, and the impasse of Standedge called for the highest, deepest and longest canal tunnel in the land, opening in 1811. Across the bridge head up the road to a junction at the former Tunnel End Inn. Climb past it, through a gate and up a path alongside a driveway. Pass left of the house above, up the tapering garden to a gate onto a rough road. Go left past several dwellings, becoming surfaced to reach a junction. Take the right option to maintain a higher course to two more houses. It ends just before the last one, where a walled footway passes to its right. Emerging onto open slopes beneath Great Edge it advances invitingly away, rising gently to a bridle-gate in a fence.

The path drops slightly, winding to the right and on past a ruin. A flagged path drops to a streamlet, across which double back a few yards to climb a wallside to a gate onto a narrow road. Turn right past Lower Green Owlers and down to a dip at Green Owlers Clough. Go left on the rough road above it to the moor edge. At a fork take the track left, remaining enclosed to rise to White Hall. Here a stile by a gate on the left sends a broad path away onto grassy moor. Haigh Clough is ahead, with March Haigh Reservoir's embankment beneath March Hill. Approaching a side-stream, ignore a right branch up to a fence corner, and keep on to cross the streamlet on stone slabs. The path now marches grandly along the rim of Haigh Clough, a near-level course until arrival at a flat, stone-arched bridge on a sidestream. Without crossing, bear right on a thinner path ascending its near side, soon going left to bridge it, and along the short way to the reservoir's outflow.

Turn left on the embankment path, rising a few feet at the far end to head away with an old catchwater, quickly meeting a broader path at a stone post inscribed 'PH Road'. Turn left for a gentle descent of the packhorse route of Rapes Highway. Passing another post, stone flags take over until just short of the head of Willykay Clough. Across this the path has further flagging before dropping into Stonepit Lee Clough. After a stonier descent to a confluence, bear right on a broader path to Close Gate Bridge. Better known as Eastergate Bridge, this graceful packhorse bridge overlooks another confluence. Across, a path runs downstream to a bridle-gate onto Blake Lea Lane. Turn right, dropping a little to level out at Hey Green House. After the terrace of Lower Hey Green, a bridle-gate on the right sends a firm path alongside the stream and a drained reservoir. At the end, drop right between a terrace and the grassy embankment to a gateway onto a road. Cross and go down a grassy area to return to Tunnel End, then retrace opening steps on the towpath.

Tunnel End, Marsden

11 PULE HILL

$3^1{}_2$ miles from Standedge

An invigorating high-level stroll on good paths throughout

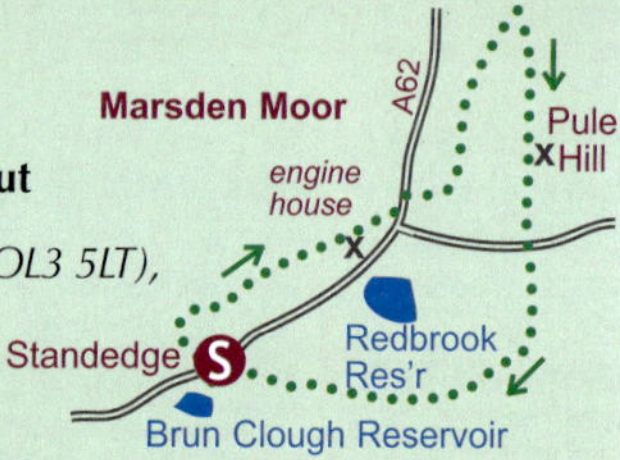

Start *Brun Clough (SE 018094; OL3 5LT), reservoir car park, A62 summit*
Map *OS Explorer OL1, Peak District, Dark Peak & Explorer OL21, South Pennines*
Access *Open Access, National Trust land*

The crest of Standedge sits on the Pennine watershed, and Brun Clough Reservoir was built to help supply the Huddersfield Narrow Canal: canal and rail tunnels run directly beneath. Across the road follow the Pennine Way north along a rough, rising track. At an early junction bear left, and shortly after absorbing the Pennine Bridleway, the Pennine Way is signed right at a kissing-gate. An inviting path ascends moor-grass slopes, and just before a kissing-gate in a fence, take a fainter path curving right. This crosses rough tracks on a short walk to a fence-stile onto Close Moss, with Pule Hill ahead. You are on the route of a turnpike road built in 1759 by the celebrated Blind Jack of Knaresborough.

Advance straight along an improving grassy path, a gentle decline becoming stone-flagged to arrive at Thieves Clough Bridge, a remarkable survivor from turnpike days. Resume on the part-flagged path down to a fork in front of spoil heaps, where remain on the flagged path dropping left with an old wall. The flags end as a grassy continuation suddenly arrives at the gaunt Redbrook engine winding-house, which helped extract spoil during tunnel construction. The path crosses the old wall to run past the ruin and down beyond the spoil heaps. Over the small embankment of a former dam, it rises pleasantly the short way to a stile onto the A62 opposite the former Carriage House pub. Cross to the verge and go left 100 yards to a fence-stile. A thin path rises pleasantly to soon join a good level path beneath Pule Hill's craggy edge.

Go left for a few minutes to a circular, red-brick air-shaft providing ventilation for the tunnels below. Alongside are the remains of another engine house. Here you meet adjacent grassy ways ascending right. Both served old quarries above, the first being an incline down which stone was carried. Whilst you could take the steeper, more direct one to the quarry site, preferably use the second, better-graded path slanting past a second air-shaft and rising grandly to the northern limit of the craggy edge. A good path doubles back right, largely set back from the edge but meeting it at the quarry's sheer rim. Resuming, you soon ease to arrive at Pule Hill's summit at 1433ft/437m, marked by a modern standing stone.

Continue your direction a few strides to the steeper edge falling away south. A well-used path drops initially steeply, then easing down to a fork just past a scrappy cairn. Slant left down onto a plateau, where a right fork takes you onto Mount Road. Cross straight over on a path running to soon join the embankment of an old catchwater drain. Keep left on this, winding around to meet the broad track of the second turnpike road over Standedge. Turn right for a gentle rise to Warcock Hill, revealing Redbrook Reservoir down to your right. This same route drops gently to pass a pool and on beneath a breached embankment. The continuing way soon rises gently across the moor, joined by a fence to reach a brow. Running to a gate at a fence junction, continue with a fence to reveal the car park just ahead.

Redbrook engine house and Pule Hill

12 HOLLINGWORTH LAKE

4¼ miles from Littleborough

Very easy walking, with streamside and towpath complementing the lake experience

Start *Heritage centre (SD 938163; OL15 0JB) behind church, roadside parking nearby*
Map *OS Explorer OL21, South Pennines*

Littleborough is an independent little place with the Rochdale Canal flowing within a stone's throw of the centre. The Heritage Centre is located in the old Coach House, a 200 year-old stabling block of the Falcon Inn. Return to Church Street outside Holy Trinity church on the main road junction, noting a tollhouse from around 1824 across it. Cross to the Halifax road, passing under the railway bridge. Turn right on Canal Street (B6225) to the canal, then go left on the towpath. At the first lock cross the bridge and quickly leave the canal on a snicket by a terrace of houses. Joining a lane, cross straight over along an access road beneath an unseen millpond. As a broad drive it runs on into the greenery of the Ealees Valley.

Remain on the track near Ealees Brook, passing a racehorse sanctuary. When it rises left at the end, go straight ahead over a streamlet and on a firm path along the open valley floor. Reaching a footbridge, cross to a broad path into the edge of Hollingworth Lake Country Park. With Ealees Pond down to the left, keep on to an access road which runs past a car park to the visitor centre with refreshments. Just past it you join a road alongside Hollingworth Lake. Cross to the footway and go left, with the M62 revealed ahead crossing 140ft high Rakewood Viaduct. After the footway ends, continue to a gated access road on the right. This leads past the nature reserve section of the lake, and later a bird-hide before the shore curves around to the Promontory with its cafe and WC.

Hollingworth Lake was long known as the 'Weighver's Seaport', a hugely popular resort for Victorian millworkers for whom the real seaside was very distant. The many attractions included boating, swimming, fishing, a 'Promenade', hotels, cafes, amusements and a steam ferry. The lake itself dates back two centuries, having been created to help supply the canal. Continue round (now unsurfaced) past an activity centre, and trace this same broad path all the way round. Over a grassy embankment it swings around beneath houses with a fine view across the water to Blackstone Edge. The B6225 is joined at the Beach Hotel at Smithy Bridge. Turn right past a sailing club and a Blackpool-like scene, passing several refreshment opportunities before regaining the lakeshore after a car park.

When the path rejoins the roadside, leave the lower lakeside option and cross to a footway. Just a few strides further as the houses end, go left on unsurfaced Heald Lane, running along to the ramshackle environs of Lower Cleggs Wood. Through the farmyard take a kissing-gate at the end, and escape straight ahead. Joining an old wall advance across the field to reveal the canal just below, quickly dropping to bridge it. Now turn right on the firm towpath amid greenery, leaving it by rising to the B6225 road bridge. Advance a short way on the footway to use an underpass beneath the railway line at the station, joining a road out front and going right to finish.

Hollingworth Lake

13 BLACKSTONE EDGE

3½ miles from Blackstone Edge

An easy, airy stroll along the tops to a landmark gritstone edge

Start *The White House (SD 968178; OL15 0LG), car park on A58 beneath pub*
Map *OS Explorer OL21, South Pennines*
Access *Open Access (tiny section), see page 4*

The isolated White House pub sits on the Pennine watershed high above Littleborough, with Blackstone Edge Reservoir behind. From the car park drop a few yards down the road to a kissing-gate on the left. A broad path rises away to the embankment of an old catchwater drain. Turn right for a super level stroll: Hollingworth Lake appears below, soon followed by the crest of Blackstone Edge itself ahead. Remain on this path all the way to a fence. On its near side rises a superb setted section of old road, long attributed to the Romans but probably dating only from packhorse times. Through the gate, cross the drain and rise away on the old way, just short of the brow arriving at a path junction at the Aiggin Stone with adjacent cairn amid boulders. This is a junction of important packhorse routes, another of which you will travel on returning from the summit. The old guidestone has been restored, and remarkably there is more of it below ground than above.

Through the bridle-gate on your right a good path heads away, dipping marginally on its obvious course for the crest of Blackstone Edge, whose summit rocks are immediately visible. The second half sees the path rising gently above the start of the edge proper to soon gain the top. An OS column at 1548ft/472m is cemented onto a mighty boulder, although the highest point would appear to be the adjacent boulders. Windfarms aplenty feature in an expansive view. Westwards you look down onto greater Manchester beyond Littleborough and Hollingworth Lake. The Summit Gorge is backed by Scout Moor, leading the eye to Pendle Hill through the Cliviger Gorge: to the north are Black Hameldon and Boulsworth Hill, and southwards the moors above Saddleworth.

Retracing steps to the Aiggin Stone, this time cross straight over the previous old way, past the stone onto a super path slanting gently left down the grassy moor. Splendid paved and embanked sections confirm this was also a valued route in packhorse times. Lower down it arrives alongside intriguing massive blocks from quarrying, then soon descends a groove between scattered rocks to emerge at an old quarry site. With the catchwater drain just below, the path quickly drops to a concrete footbridge across it. Turn right to quickly return to the path dropping back to the start.

For a more varied finish however, continue along the now grassy drain-side track. Above a solitary house pass through a bridle-gate, and with Blackstone Edge Reservoir just across the road, follow this pleasant course, bridging the drain to reach a tunnel entrance just past a drain junction. While the track doubles back around the tunnel to a gate onto the road, instead advance further on a grassy little path, with a drain returning for company to arrive at a small pool. Here a stile on the left puts you onto the road at the B6138 Mytholmroyd junction. Cross to the footway outside the reservoir and go left back to the pub, passing the Pennine Way gate beneath the dam en route.

On Blackstone Edge

14 Scammonden Water

4¼ miles from Scammonden

A relaxing circuit of an iconic reservoir

Start *Scammonden (SE 055162; HD3 3FR), Yorkshire Water's Scammonden Reservoir car park off A640 near Pole Moor*
Map *OS Explorer OL21, South Pennines*

With extensive views over the reservoir, from the car park's far end a gate sends a firm, broad path parallel to the road. At an early fork, use either as they run through trees to rejoin. Reaching a bend alongside the road, turn sharp left down into deeper trees. Shortly after a sharp dog-leg it forks: take the level right branch to quickly gain the embankment end beneath the M62. Cross the dam on a broad path just a fence away from thundering waggons. Opened in 1971, the Trans-Pennine motorway was a major engineering feat that earned greatest recognition in its bridging of the Scammonden valley: it combined a new reservoir with a 249ft high dam, carrying the motorway towards its summit on the Lancashire border.

At the end bear left on a broad, firm path into trees, rising from the shore to open out beneath a steep, heathery bank. It runs on to reach a stone hut, with Deanhead church just above. Here, as the path prepares to drop away, fork right on a path rising to quickly enter the little hamlet of Deanhead. Advance to School House just ahead, then go left on a grassy track along the rear of redundant St Bartholomew's church. Just above are the gritstone cliffs of Scar Rocks. At the end of the churchyard is a fork. Bear left, a good path angling gently down to run a level course through trees. Past a pond you emerge into the open, with the upper section of the reservoir below and big moorland views ahead.

Advance on beneath a steep, heathery bank, soon forking where the left branch drops away. Remain on the upper path, above a fence beneath new plantings in the heather to reach a kissing-gate. The path then rises slightly above a wood to a stile onto New Lane. Go briefly left to a sharp bend, where go straight ahead to a gate sending a level path away with a fence. With Deanhead Reservoir just ahead beneath remote moors, the path quickly runs to its embankment. Cross the stile/gate and follow the grassy embankment path. The reservoir was completed in 1836 to supply textile mills: across it are the folds of Deanhead Moor. Having bridged the outflow take the rough road down to a stile/gate back onto New Lane, and turn left to a car park.

Pass into the recreation area, and a firm path runs along the bottom to enter trees alongside Black Burne Brook. Ignoring an early footbridge, keep on to the head of Scammonden Water. The path runs pleasantly by the shore to soon reach an impasse at a slipway. A stiff pull right quickly joins an access road: go left the short way towards a scouts' activity centre. Without entering, take a broad path slanting right through colourful surrounds. Within a couple of minutes, fork left to a bridle-gate above a sailing clubhouse at the old vicarage. A little further, it drops steeply back to the shore to commence a sustained easy stroll. Ignoring a right branch uphill at an early fork by a sculpture, continue to a fork with an underpass visible just ahead. A tablet by the valve tower ahead recalls the lake's opening by Queen Elizabeth II. Bear right, climbing briefly steeply to rejoin the outward route to finish

Scammonden Water

15 Ryburn Valley

3¾ miles from Ripponden

Riverbank and reservoir in the uppermost Ryburn Valley

Start *Village centre (SE 040197; HX6 4DF), Royd Lane car park*
Map *OS Explorer OL21, South Pennines*

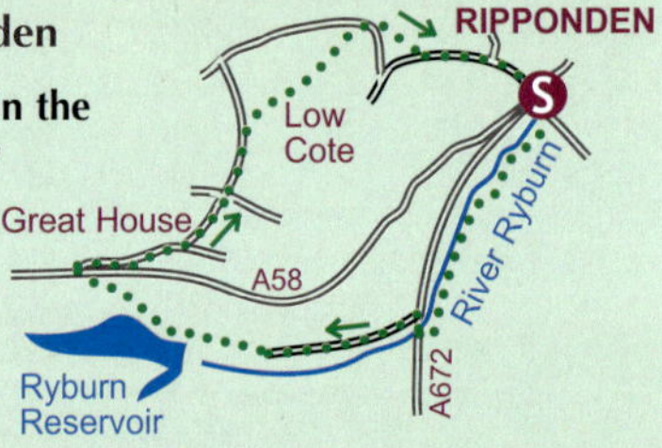

Ripponden village has St Bartholomew's tall church spire rising above a packhorse bridge and the historic Old Bridge Inn. From the church cross neither bridge, but pass between houses at Mill Fold at Bridge End and underneath the main road bridge over the River Ryburn. A setted road heads upstream, then pass through a small park onto a road. Advance along its riverside course, and beyond houses and a small industrial site a surfaced drive runs along the riverbank. When this ends at Ellis Bottom Farm, a path takes over to trace the Ryburn through a super woodland section. Reaching a footbridge, don't cross but take a few stone steps up to resume through trees. Ignore too a branch left up to a bridge over the former railway. The path drops back down and on above a steep plunge to the Ryburn to reach a confluence. Just to the left, inflowing Booth Dean Beck leads you to a road: turn right to bridge the beck up onto the A672 at Slitheroe Bridge.

Use the main road to cross the Ryburn and go left on Bar Lane, parallel with the river. This runs upstream to its eventual demise at housing on a mill site. En route much housing is passed, then a millpond on the left and a hidden one on the right. A setted road takes over to climb to a hairpin bend: pass left of an old garage, onto a path with a millpond below and Ryburn Reservoir's dam in front. Continuing, steps climb to emerge alongside the dam. Largely surrounded by woodland, the reservoir blends well into its deep fold of the valley: ahead is the massive Baitings Dam.

Cross the access road to a few steps rising to a stile, then left on a grassy path above the reservoir to a stile/gate into trees. Leave this permissive path within five minutes, just before a wall comes down from the right. Here a path rises 30 yards up to adjacent fence-stiles. A path runs left with a fence, soon leaving it to slant up across a more open, scrubby bank. It rises away with an old wall on your left and increasingly grand views over the reservoir. Further, it swings right to the top, then through an old gateway runs left with the wall past a stone trough. Becoming briefly enclosed, pass through a small gate and continue with the wall up to a couple of houses, and up the short access road onto the A58.

Cross and head away on narrow Hollin Lane, rising gently away. Keep left at a fork where it enjoys a setted spell, now as Great House Lane passing impressive Great House. Easing out to reach a crossroads, go straight across on Green Lane. Over a gentle brow it drops to a staggered junction with old lanes: go right down the walled track of Cote Road. On the left you pass the old house of Low Cote, and further, a drive comes in to run to another road. Cross over behind a house, over a second road and along an enclosed cart track. When it turns sharp left just past a house, advance over open ground. Just down the wallside, a narrow path soon becomes enclosed to descend to cottages on Royd Lane. Dropping steeply into the centre, cross the main road and down a short lane to the pub and packhorse bridge.

Old Bridge Inn

16 NORLAND MOOR

4 miles from Norland

A colourful stroll around a popular pocket moorland

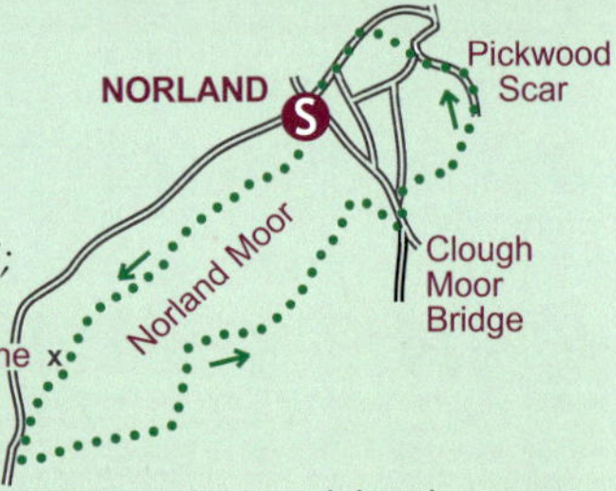

Start *Village centre (SE 065225; HX6 3RN), crossroads of Shaw Lane, Clough Road and Berry Moor Road by war memorial: car park off Shaw Lane, along short track by play area at corner of moor.* ***Map*** *OS Explorer OL21, South Pennines*

Scattered Norland 'Town' is a hilltop settlement boasting splendid centuries-old clothiers' houses: some are revealed later. Norland Moor is an island-like heather tract high above Sowerby Bridge, bearing much-healed scars of small-scale quarrying. From the car park take a broad path rising diagonally away to heathery old quarries on the brow. Forking within 50 strides, keep left to rise to a crossroads with a broader path. Turn right to rise very gently across the moor, passing above old quarry sites and along a gentle but obvious edge. Beyond a covered reservoir where the Calderdale Way departs left, the more extensive old quarries of Turgate Delph are passed. Forging on above them, the main path bears left to an Ordnance Survey column at 931ft/284m. At the junction here turn right to regain the edge at the distinctive Ladstone Rock, with extensive views west over the Ryburn Valley.

Resuming along the edge, the path soon drops towards the road. Without setting foot on tarmac, advance straight on a parallel path to the moor corner, with chalets behind. Here take a clear path left to remain on the moor edge, rising by a wall. It soon veers gently away to a junction at an outer wall corner. Now bear right on the splendid wallside path's very gentle decline through colourful vegetation. Reaching another corner, an enclosed way runs straight on, but you go left to again remain on the moor.

Initially between walls, it drops slightly to another outer corner. At this cross-paths go right to resume as before, on a broader path again gently declining with the boundary wall to your right. Ignore a branch left and remain on the path near the moor edge, curving left to absorb the Calderdale Way path at a solid cairn.

Keep on to the wall corner near the edge of the moor. At this cross-paths, under a pylon, turn right over a streamlet to a road junction at Clough Moor Bridge: note the old boundary stone set into it. Don't cross but go left a few strides on the road, then bear right on a minor open road. After 60 yards bear right on a good, level path, nearing a wall and soon arriving at a path junction by the wall. Turn right on the enclosed old way of Dye House Lane dropping into trees, slanting left pleasantly down to a house at the hamlet of Pickwood Scar. Advance along the road out to reach a junction at a house, where steps on the left send a short, setted path up to a stile. The path climbs the field to another stile, then slants faintly up to a gate in the top right corner. A green lane runs the few strides right onto Norland Town Road opposite Upper Old Hall. Outstanding just down to the right is Lower Old Hall, with a 1634 datestone. Go left up past the former Blue Ball Inn and Fallingworth Hall dated 1642. At a junction turn right on Berry Moor Road to finish.

The Ryburn Valley from Norland Moor

17 NORTH DEAN WOOD

3¼ miles from West Vale

Beautiful woodland on the edge of Greetland

Start *Bow Bridge (SE 096213; HX4 8AN), Brig Royd car park at crossroads*
Map *OS Explorer OL21, South Pennines*

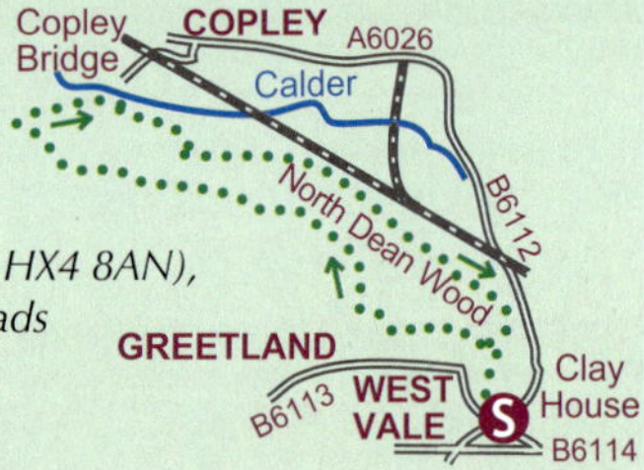

At the rear of the car park is a footbridge into Clayhouse Park: bear right towards Clay House, part hidden by trees. A path drops to a lower grassy area, and steps to the left ascend through gardens to this fine 17th century house. Between the house and its aisled barn, a few steps to the left take you up a grassy area to a broad track behind a wall-gap on the edge of woodland. Turning left a couple of paces, bear right off the track to a wall-stile ahead sending a path rising through trees. With a tall fence on your left, when this quickly ends take the level path left, emerging at the head of an access track. In the corner ahead, an enclosed setted path ascends to an access track. Go left, becoming a grassy cart track above terraced housing. At the last of these take a path right into trees, and crossing a track it climbs to a minor road in front of a house.

Go right the short way to a junction, and double back left on an access road between houses. Quickly reaching a junction, go right. This walled track heads away between fields, improving to a cart track approaching North Dean Wood. The final short section is a narrow footway into the wood top, going left on a sustained amble above steep woods and craggy bluffs. Rising very gradually, ignore all branches to eventually join a rough road. Just half a minute to the right is a junction where the road slants down into trees, a drive goes left, and the way resumes along the wood top. Ignore all of these in favour of the right-most option, a clear path dropping right of the road. It runs a splendid sunken course down the wood, passing above a cottage. At its far wall corner a stone flight sends a short-cut path down onto rough North Dean Road.

Turn right, slanting at a steady angle all the way down outside the wood to Copley's gaunt, redundant St Stephen's church. Before commencing the return, advance a few paces to appraise an octagonal 1830s tollhouse, with rebuilt Copley Bridge on the River Calder. Back at the church, a stile on the right sends a level path above it. Immediately forking, take the gently ascending right branch. When this quickly forks, remain on the level left option. With steep slopes above, this rises only slightly to quickly arrive at the edge of a murky pool. Across its minimal outflow ascend steps to a path junction, then rise right up further steps to a guidepost. This sends you back right up to another junction on a bouldery knoll. Go left to commence a near-level stride for a considerable time.

Further, a more open section runs through bracken to re-enter trees at the end. The path runs above a boundary wall, rising marginally through colourful surrounds as a broad path merges from the right beneath further crags. A little beyond is a fork on a brow beneath a sizeable crag: as the broader left option drops gently away, remain on the thinner but very clear level path ahead. Merging into a broader track rising from the left, this surmounts a minor brow, and on through an old quarry site to a gate behind a house. Just beyond, you join its access track to find yourself back on the outward route. Descend the setted footway on your left and down the rough road below to cross onto the grass at Clay House.

Copley Viaduct and Wainhouse Tower from North Dean Wood

18 OVENDEN MOOR

4 miles from Ogden

Rugged moorland above a popular reservoir

Start *Ogden Water (SE 066308; HX2 8XZ), car park on Ogden Lane off A629, Causeway Foot*
Map *OS Explorer OL21, South Pennines*

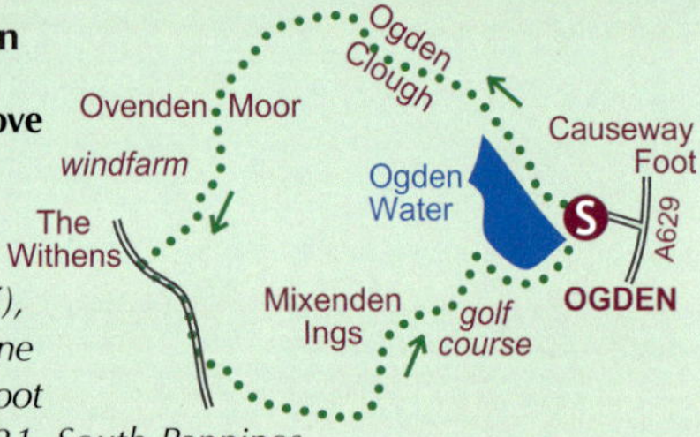

Ogden Water has a visitor centre with refreshments and WC. At the end of the lower car park a kissing-gate sends a broad path into trees. Absorbing another, it angles towards the reservoir, meeting a lower, level path just short of the end. Near its head you reach a footbridge on a side dam. While the reservoir circuit path crosses it, your way is straight ahead, a thinner path that within a minute meets a broader one coming in from the right. Bear left on it, and ignoring an early left fork downhill, forge on, rising gently before dropping to run tightly with the lively beck. The end of the wood is quickly reached, and a stile sends a path into the open country of Ogden Clough.

Remain on your bank as footbridges offer a south bank option. This steep-walled clough is a little gem, and the path soon reaches twin waterfalls as the peaty moorland stream negotiates gritstone ledges. At the second falls the path rises to a junction by a sturdy bridge over a little dam: immediately upstream are gritstone crags. Across this waterworks bridge a path rises away to a stile onto the heathery sweep of Ovenden Moor. Its 23 100ft wind turbines from 1993 were replaced by 9 270ft ones in 2016. Shadowed by a fence to the left, a broad path heads towards them, rising gently to a brow with the turbines almost within touching distance. The path drops to bridge Skirden Clough, then rises as a broader track to a kissing-gate onto the firm Withens New Road. Turn right to a kissing-gate onto Cold Edge Road at The Withens. Built in 1862 to serve quarrymen, until 21st century closure it was West Yorkshire's highest pub.

Go left for a few minutes on the steadily declining road, with views right over Cold Edge Dams into Luddenden. Shortly after a drive on the right, a kissing-gate on the left sends a faint way away right, crossing to a distinct bank and ditch with a fence behind. Go right on this the short way to a corner stile in a wall, and drop left between old walls. The right one ends before your faint way slowly leaves the left-hand wall to curve to a kissing-gate in a sturdy wall on the right. The way drops a few yards further to the head of a broad, old green way. Advance halfway along to a gateway in the left-hand wall, and double back left on a thin trod. This drops slightly to pass through an old wall and across to a kissing-gate at a wall junction onto a grassy corner of Ovenden Moor.

Follow the wall away until it turns off, then a fence shadows the thin path to the edge of steeper slopes above the colourful hollow of Mixenden Ings occupied by a golf course. The thin path descends to a stile onto it, and yellow-topped marker posts will guide you across. Across a fairway bear gently left on a grass track, over a cross-paths to a substantial bridge on the central stream. A short way further, a thin path scales the slope alongside a bracken patch, slanting right and broadening as you gain height along the bracken fringe. On the brow, shortly turn left to cross two more fairways to rejoin Withens New Road by the reservoir plantation. Turn right to drop to the dam, crossing it to finish.

Ogden Water

19 LUDDENDEN DEAN

4¼ miles from Luddenden

A quite demanding exploration of a colourful side valley

Start *Village centre (SE 041261; HX2 6PX), car park/WC at southern end on Luddenden Lane*
Map *OS Explorer OL21, South Pennines*

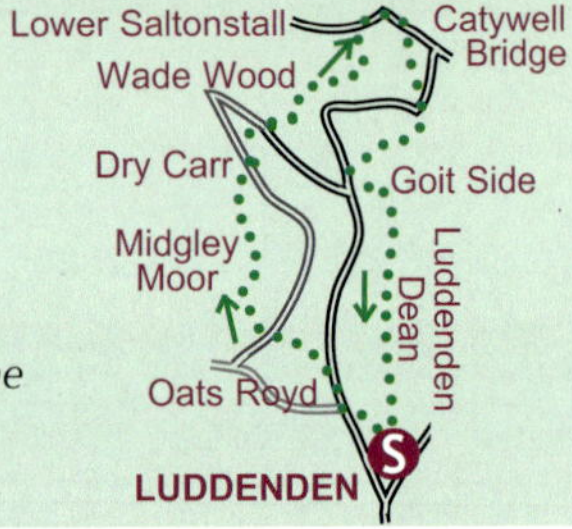

Characterful Luddenden is based around the Lord Nelson pub, across a tiny square from the church. From the war memorial take the road above the pub to the foot of Old Lane, by a former school. The setted lane climbs steeply to a crossroads, where turn right for a few minutes towards Oats Royd Mill with its tall chimney. Immediately before Oats Royd House, turn left up setted Delph Hill Lane. Past houses it becomes grassier, climbing to a junction with a rough lane from the left. Continue up onto another road, crossing to ascend Radcliffe Lane. Swinging right above a house, it quickly ends at Brownhill Farm. Continue up a grassy way beneath heathery moorland, quickly reaching a stile onto Midgley Moor.

Turn right on the wallside path with glorious views, and after a fence takes over, a stile in it accesses a parallel farm road. Go left, slanting down a hairpin at the end of High House Lane, where go right the few yards to Dry Carr Lane. Double back left down it, and at the third house (attractive Dry Carr), double back down its short drive. A small gate at the yard corner sends a faint way left down a wallside, through an old gateway to a stile into a small wood. The path continues the short way down to emerge behind a house onto Jerusalem Lane. Turn right to a stile at the start of Wade Wood, from where a path slants down to a small gate in a wall-gap, below which cross Wade Bridge on Luddenden Brook.

Take a path rising half-right: at an early level junction double back left uphill, quickly reaching another junction. Take the path climbing right, initially stepped then slanting right to pass between twin boulders at the wood top. Through a wall-stile/gate into a field, go right a few strides to a stile in the ascending wall, then a path crosses to a corner wall-stile. From another beyond, trace a wall beneath Lower Saltonstall to a stile/gate at the end. Turn up the wallside into the hamlet, going straight up onto a road then right to the Cat-i-the-Well pub. Across Catywell Bridge just past it, as the road rises away take a drive right after the trees to a house at Hock Cliff. Passing to its left via small gates into a broadening field, a thin path contours across the right side of the field. Initially by a wall, it runs pleasantly on to a stile onto Bank House Lane.

Rise a few paces left, then double back right down setted Holme House Lane. Past houses it narrows to a footway, broadening to an access road as it doubles back right past houses back onto Bank House Lane. Drop left to bridge Luddenden Brook, then turn left along an access road to houses at Goit Side. Advance on to a cobbled fork at characterful houses, then bear left, and straight on the broad track. This runs to two final houses, where the bridleway continues into trees to soon emerge at another row of houses. At the end the access road goes left over the brook, but your way is straight on, soon narrowing back to a bridleway. Its firm course in the company of Luddenden Brook runs to a fork just short of the village, and either option will suffice.

Luddenden Dean

20 CRAGG VALE

4¼ miles from Mytholmroyd

Cragg Vale's charms include much delightful woodland

Start *Village centre (SE 012260; HX7 5DS), car park by church*
Map *OS Explorer OL21, South Pennines*

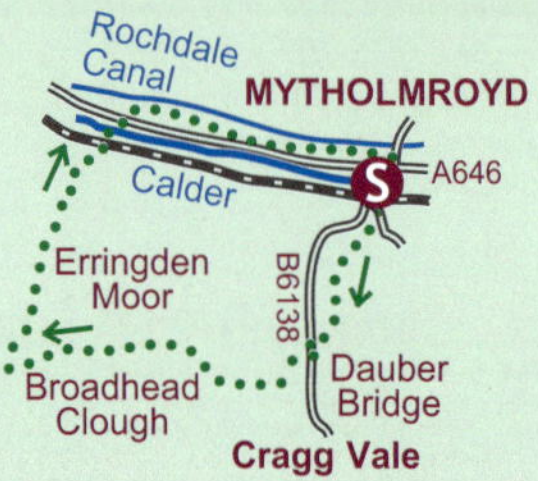

Mytholmroyd has the Dusty Miller pub and shops where Cragg Brook joins the River Calder. Cross the bridge on the B6138 (with parallel footbridge), along New Road passing under the rail bridge. Opposite the Shoulder of Mutton bear left on Scout Road, with 17th century Mytholmroyd Farmhouse on the left. At once turn sharply right up Hall Bank Lane at a former Methodist church. When it turns left just above, bear right up a suburban road to its far end. An enclosed path takes over above a steep wooded bank, curving left into open woodland. Remaining on the wood top, the path runs on to leave at a stile at the end of the business park above. Without joining the access road, turn right on an enclosed path outside the wood. Emerging into a field at the end, continue to a corner stile, from where steep steps drop to the B6138.

Cross to the footway and go briefly right to Dauber Bridge, then double back left on an unsurfaced access road close by Cragg Brook. It swings right to rise alongside a wooded clough, and leaving the stream it forks. Bear left, running on into Spring Wood via a cattle-grid. Forking again, use neither but take a path straight ahead into Broadhead Clough nature reserve. Initially flagged, it winds on and steadily upwards into deep woodland. Steep steps lead to easier progress and a gentle ascent near the wood edge. Shortly after a fence comes in on the right, cross via a kissing-gate from where the path climbs back right. Within just a few feet it gains the rim of the amphitheatre on the edge of Erringden Moor.

A thin path heads directly away across open moor, and from a crumbling wall corner it runs a straight, near-level course with the vestiges of a wall. Evading moist moments, a wall corner is reached at the end. At this cross-paths head straight on with the wall on your right, skirting a pool to another corner just ahead. Leaving the wall, slant gently left (no path) to drop to a stile in a moor-bottom fence. Through a crumbling wall behind, you start the long descent alongside a sunken way. This leads down to the cart track of Haven Lane. At a stile a few steps to the right, resume the descent on a path slanting back left down through colourful country.

The path runs down towards a pylon, and beneath it swings left towards the edge of trees. Along their fringe it turns downhill again, then slants right to a stile onto an access road. From a stile opposite, a path drops by a wooded stream. Through a stile at the bottom, drop into a sheep pasture to a corner stile, beneath which is a slab bridge at a tiny confluence. Bear left across the field to a stile/gate onto a walled access lane in front of trees. Turn right, keeping left past Carr House. It becomes surfaced to cross railway and river onto the A646. Cross to the Rochdale Canal towpath, and turn right for a short walk back into Mytholmroyd. Passing a lock and beneath a couple of stone-arched bridges, leave by steps up onto a modern road bridge. Turn right down Midgley Road, with the start just to the right.

Mytholmroyd Farmhouse

21 HEPTONSTALL

3¼ miles from Hebden Bridge

A steep haul to a classic old village, with dramatic views

Start *Bridge Gate (SD 992273; HX7 8EX), town centre car parks*
Map *OS Explorer OL21, South Pennines*

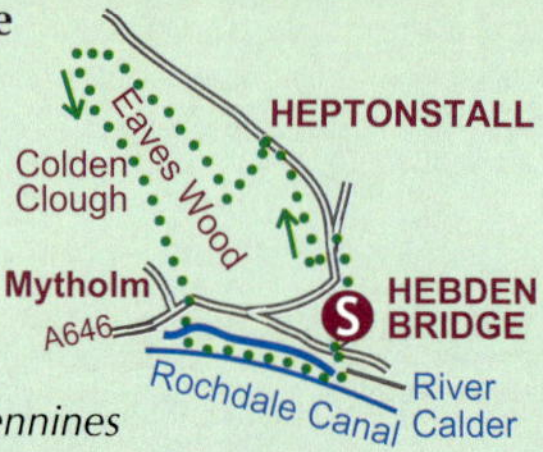

Hebden Bridge is the focal point of Upper Calderdale, its houses climbing alarmingly steeply up hillsides above the meeting of two valleys. The lively centre boasts canal trips, independent shops, a marina on the Rochdale Canal, the Little Theatre, an iconic cinema, the Trades Club music venue and a summer arts festival. From Bridge Gate cross the stone-arched packhorse bridge on Hebden Water and cross the road to The Buttress, a relentlessly steep, setted old way. Joining a road at the top, go briefly left to an old milestone at a junction, then ascend an access road opposite. Beyond the second house it ends at a small quarry site, just before which a part enclosed path heads off right. Rising gently through part wooded surrounds, it curves up to emerge via the front of a short terrace onto a road at the foot of Heptonstall. Turn left up past the Post office/shop and tearoom.

Heptonstall is a fascinating hilltop village, a veritable timewarp in which its weather-beaten stone cottages revel. Focal point is the churchyard separating the Victorian church from the old church of St Thomas a'Becket, partly dating from the 13th century. Alongside is the old grammar school of 1772, now a museum. There are two pubs, the Cross Inn and the White Lion. Leave the main street by an enclosed path to the museum on the left, between the pubs. Entering the old churchyard advance to the new church, and a path goes left out onto a rough lane. Bear right on this, quickly crossing a suburban road. Just a little further at a fork, ignore the cart track bearing left and take the surfaced path ahead. This runs between more gardens, over another road then escapes to emerge onto the crest of Eaves Wood. This reveals dramatic views from airy gritstone outcrops above Colden Clough, take care! Stoodley Pike is seen from valley floor to its towering monument.

Turn right on a super, high-level path above the clough. Keeping to the upper path, the later stages feature a gentle clamber through the bouldery wood top before joining an access road. Turn down this a short way, and at old troughs ignore a level path right. Just below, double back left on a path into trees. It drops steeply past a cottage, then pleasantly down along the wood edge. It soon levels out to run a nice, broad course along the base of Eaves Wood. At the end the main way drops down through a gate, on a briefly enclosed course down onto an access road at Mytholm. Go left on this, quickly diverted around the right side of the end house, above a steep wooded bank opposite the gaunt church. At the end continue through the trees to a junction, where your path slants down onto the A646. Go briefly right and cross at an island after bridging Colden Water, then turn down steps on an urban footpath shadowing the beck to its confluence with the River Calder. A footbridge over this leads straight ahead onto the canal towpath. Turn left to quickly return, bridging the Calder to double back left down onto Holme Street, back into the centre.

The old church of St Thomas a'Becket, Heptonstall

22 Hardcastle Crags

3¾ miles from Midgehole

Renowned woodland on the outskirts of Hebden Bridge

Start *New Bridge (SD 988291; HX7 7AL), National Trust's Hardcastle Crags car park*
Map *OS Explorer OL21, South Pennines*

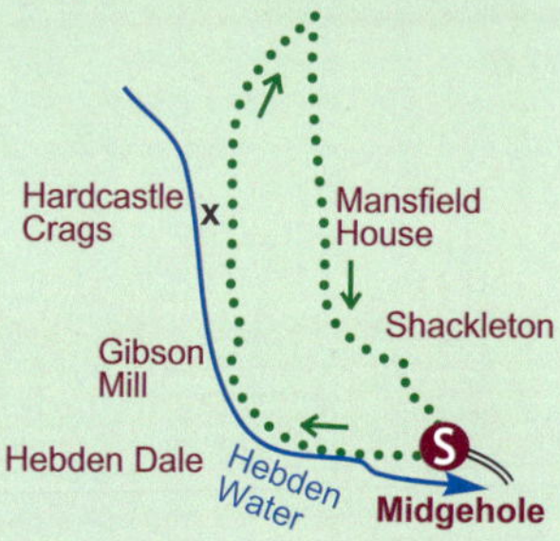

Hardcastle Crags is the universal name for richly-wooded Hebden Dale, through which flows Hebden Water. From the lower car park head up the drive a few strides until just past a lodge, then fork left on a path dropping to Hebden Water. Here a wide path is met and accompanied upstream for almost a mile and a quarter to Gibson Mill. The first of two impasses is quickly reached as the path slants back right a little to run a parallel course above the beck. Soon forking, one drops back to the beck to return a little later, or you could simply remain on this level one higher above the bank. Having merged, the path now runs on to quickly drop back to the beck to commence a delectable stroll upstream. Further, the path is forced slightly up again in two near parallel sections, to run on again a little higher to soon reach a T-junction: drop left the short way to a clearing alongside stepping-stones. A now unbroken stroll leads upstream to the mill, passing further stepping-stones.

Restored by the National Trust, Gibson Mill was founded in 1800 as a water-powered cotton mill. It ceased to operate in the 1890s, becoming a dance hall and a roller-skating rink in the mid-20th century. With a cafe, shop, information and exhibitions, it is is now at the forefront of sustainable technology, producing its own power by solar and water. Around the back is a millpond, while related features include a row of workers' cottages and a stone-arched bridge spanning the beck to a WC. Join the adjacent driveway to climb above the beck, within a few minutes reaching a branch path signed left to 'The Crags'. This demands a short detour winding up onto a pronounced spur, quickly ascending to the steep rise of Hardcastle Crags. This modest grouping of rock outcrops occupies a prominent knoll bedecked with clumps of heather, with a slender ridge rising above the treetops.

Continuing on from the crags, remain on the main track as it swings uphill to merge with a firmer access road at the wood top. Turn right for a long, easy stroll to the hamlet of Shackleton, where immediately before the first building take a gate on the right. Dropping away towards wooded Hebden Dale, a narrow, grassy way forms between old walls, down to a stile at the bottom into the top of Foul Scout Wood. Firstly go a few strides right onto the crest of Willow Gate Rock, a splendid viewpoint. Back at the stile, take the path dropping left to rapidly reach a path junction. Keep left, slanting down what is largely a splendid stone causeway amid scattered boulders. This drops steadily through the wood to the corner of a large open pasture. Keeping above it you quickly leave the trees to become pleasantly enclosed, still largely on the old causey. At the bottom it empties you back into the wood, with the main car park just below.

Hebden Water

23 CRIMSWORTH DEAN

3½ miles from Midgehole

An easy walk around a hugely colourful side valley, with super woodland and beck scenery

Start *New Bridge (SD 988291; HX7 7AL), National Trust's Hardcastle Crags car park*
Map *OS Explorer OL21, South Pennines*

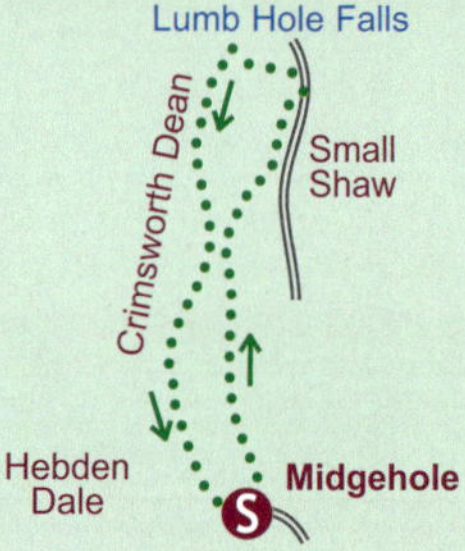

From the car park return across the bridge and take a narrow way climbing behind the WC. At a solitary house, leave through a gate on the left, a grassy track rising steadily away across open pastures. After a spell between walls it narrows to a path, and at the far end squeezes beneath a dam wall into trees at the start of a series of millponds at Middle Dean. Go left with a drain, opening out to trace a dry dam followed by fuller ones. Remain on here to an abrupt end alongside a bridge on now adjacent Crimsworth Dean Beck. Don't cross, but bear right through an old iron fence. The path slants up to a wall, rising briefly steeply to a level path at a stile out of the trees. This sends a path across colourful pasture, through a small gate where flags ease a moist section, then across to a stile into the grounds of Wheat Ing. The flagged path runs to a small gate into the garden proper. Passing right of the house, follow its drive steeply up the valley side with big views.

At a hairpin go straight on a thin path into trees, slanting up to a wall-stile into a field. Slanting right, the path fades but points to the opposite wall. Ascend to its very top outer corner, from where a stile sends you left across field-tops. Passing Upper Small Shaw you approach the next house, Barker Cote. Having swapped wallsides en route, don't enter its yard but keep on to a stile onto its drive just short of the field corner. It immediately turns up onto a road 50 yards higher, but the true path endures a complicated two minutes by taking a stile ahead into the grounds of Gib. Rise a few yards right to cross the drive to a gate, then left across a small paddock to a second small gate on the left. This sends a briefly enclosed way along the rear of the house, emerging to advance a few yards further onto Haworth Old Road. Go briefly left to an enclosed path descending steeply to Crimsworth Dean Beck. Turning right at the bottom to Lumb Bridge and Lumb Hole Falls, the packhorse bridge and waterfalls form a delectable scene.

Across the bridge a path rises downstream, but as the main path climbs steeply right between walls, pass through an old gateway in front onto a narrower path. Remaining parallel with the beck, the path contours through bracken-filled pastures to a wall-stile at the end. Passing the rear of Outwood, follow its drive to a gate into woodland. Ignore this however in favour of a gap to its left, and a part-flagged path slants down the field to a stile into trees. A path runs down to stone-arched Weet Ing Bridge: don't cross but continue on, rising a little then running towards a gate into a field. Shortly before it however, rise right on a path slanting to join a rough access road. Follow this left all the way back down to Midgehole. Early open views are enjoyed, and beyond an old quarry a firmer access road comes in. Into trees this becomes surfaced for the final stage.

Lumb Hole Falls

24 JUMBLE HOLE CLOUGH

4¾ miles from Blackshaw Head

Hillside tracks, towpath and a fascinating little side valley

Start *Hamlet centre (SD 958275; HX7 7JY), roadside parking on Hebden Bridge road*
Map *OS Explorer OL21, South Pennines*

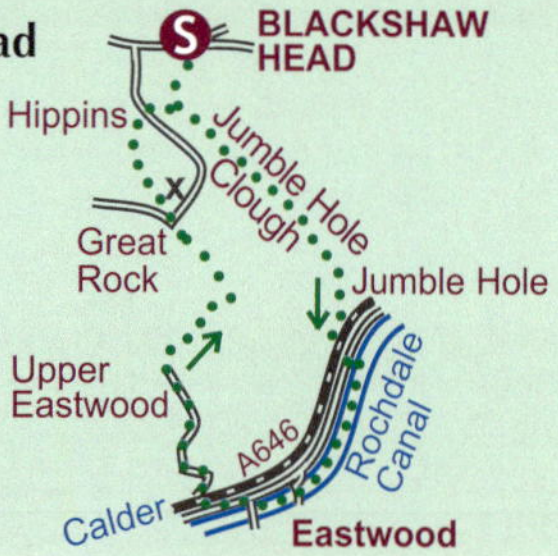

At 1115ft/340m, the walk's start is its high point. From an old milestone at the central junction, head east to the end of the chapel graveyard. Turn right down a short drive, forking right to a lower house. To its right, a stone causey descends a wallside into reedy pasture. At the house below, take the left-hand stile into a garden edge. Down the house side a causey descends a fieldside onto a drive. Across, the path drops between fields to a stile at another house. Down its side a short enclosed way drops to Hippins, a fine old house with a 1656 datestone. Immediately before it, a kissing-gate sends a wallside path left. By a stile in the wall, a path branches right, down steps to a footbridge in Jumble Hole Clough. Turn down to ruinous Staups Mill amid waterfalls and gritstone.

From here the path rises briefly, but quickly take a signed left fork to remain parallel with but high above the lively beck. Passing above a substantial crag, the super path descends to an angled cross-paths then on beneath a field, returning into denser trees to meet a drive. Go left, dropping steeply to double back to bridge the beck to a junction. Go right, the rough road shadowing the beck past mill ruins to houses at Jumble Hole. Before them cross a footbridge on the right into a field, tracing the right side up to a brow, with big views to Stoodley Pike. Continue to a corner at Mulcture Hall, where a small gate into the garden sends you across the grass to an access road. Turn down to the next hairpin, then go right on a path between railway and trees. Very quickly take a footbridge over the line down onto the A646 at Eastwood. Cross to Burnt Acres Lane, bridging the River Calder to gain the Rochdale Canal at another bridge: turn right for a towpath stroll with the river as close companion. A road interrupts at Holmcoat Bridge and Lock, then on past a cricket ground to reach Stoodley Bridge. Under this turn right onto an access road, going left over the Calder to Victoria Terrace, and rising left back onto the A646.

Cross to the footway and go left to turn right up East Lee Lane under a rail arch. Rising steeply above a wooded clough, it eases out to slant up between fields to impressive Lower East Lee, then up to fork into access roads at another house. Bear right behind it, but leave at once by an enclosed path left of the drive. Rising to houses, take steps right onto a grassy area behind them, crossing to a stile into a field. Head away to another, and a fence leads on through two gateways then along a wall top to a stile onto an access road. Turn up this for a steep, lengthy pull to a road beneath the mighty Great Rock on its heathery common. A green lane to its left rises to a gate, then along to a stile onto heathery Staups Moor. A path continues with the right-hand wall, dropping to a corner stile across a track. An initially faint path drops down a rough pasture to a stile onto a road at Hippins Bridge. Cross and turn right on the short drive to Hippins to retrace opening steps.

Great Rock

25 STOODLEY PIKE

3¼ miles from Lumbutts

A bracing high-level stroll to an iconic hilltop landmark

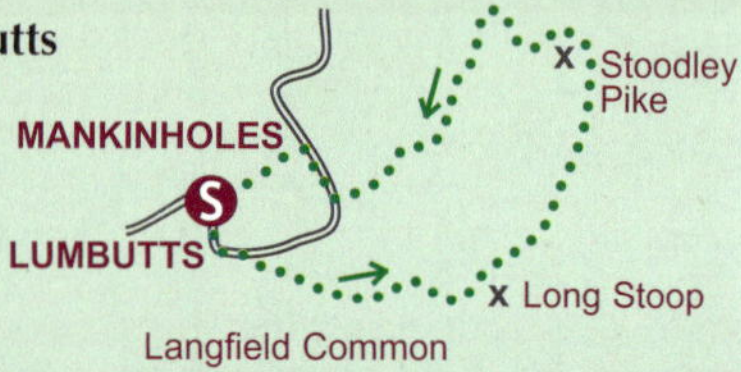

Start *Hamlet centre (SD 957233; OL14 6JB), roadside parking between pub and chapel*
Map *OS Explorer OL21, South Pennines*

Lumbutts nestles in a hollow dominated by a water wheel tower that served a cotton mill. Immediately above it is Lee Dam, one of three hovering above the hamlet. From the sprawling Top Brink Inn follow the road rising past the tower, out of the hamlet to a bend by the Methodist church. Here take a walled track right, rapidly swinging uphill on an unerring climb (latterly flagged) to a gate onto the foot of Langfield Common. Here a magnificent flagged packhorse trod rises away with a wall. When the wall parts company the way slants ever upwards across the moor, enjoying fine views to the monument and across the valley. Near the top it doubles back right to a path crossroads with the Pennine Way, overseen by the monumental Long Stoop guidepost.

Abandon the flags and turn left on the path rising gently past the stoop, up past boulders through an old quarry and following a broad and popular level course past clusters of rocks along to the Stoodley Pike monument. Erected in 1815 to celebrate peace after victory over Napoleon, it later collapsed and was replaced in 1856. An inscription over the door explains some of its history. It stands a mighty 120 feet above the 1312ft/400m moortop, and is upper Calderdale's most famous landmark. A dark, spiral staircase climbs 39 steps to a viewing balcony: the 360-degree panorama features moorland skylines in almost every direction.

Leave by a broad path departing the edge just a few yards west of the monument. This drops briefly away then slants left across the steep slopes, before long turning sharp right, and forking. Take the right option, dropping down a short groove to merge with another path. Go right down this to drop pleasantly onto a broad, firm bridle-path along the moor-foot. The housing of Harvelin Park below occupies the site of two Victorian hospitals that closed in 1987. Turning left, this old track known as London Road runs a long, largely level course along the foot of the common beneath the Pike's steep slopes. Eventually reaching a corner, through the gate ahead a walled track runs on to drop down to the edge of Mankinholes. Alongside is a floral corner featuring two stone sheep, a Millennium stone and a seat.

Turn right through the intriguing old handloom weaving settlement, passing some impressive water troughs recalling its importance in packhorse days, and a small youth hostel in a fine old building. Beyond the last buildings you quickly reach a lone house, a former Wesleyan Methodist Sunday School of 1833. The chapel itself was demolished in 1979, while alongside is a burial ground. Here turn left down the splendidly paved Lumbutts Lane to emerge back at the Top Brink. At the very foot of the lane is an old guidepost inscribed 'Halifax' and 'Heptonstall', complete with mileages.

Stoodley Pike above Mankinholes

26 REDDYSHORE SCOUT

4½ miles from Walsden

Superb walking through the impressive surrounds of the Walsden Gorge

Start *Village centre (SD 934219; OL14 6SW), roadside parking near church*
Map *OS Explorer OL21, South Pennines*

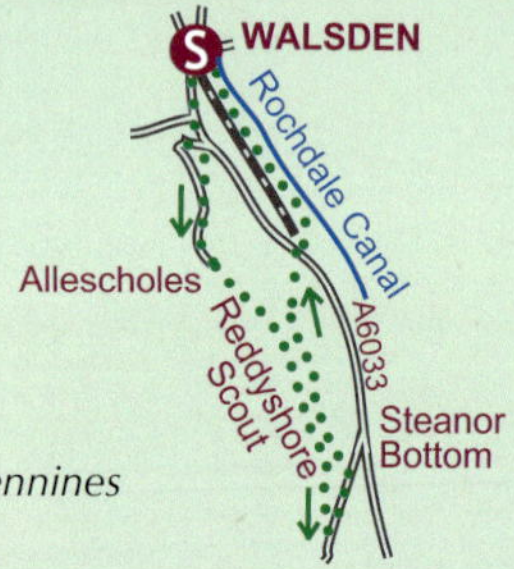

Walsden is Todmorden's southerly offshoot, occupying the narrow valley of Walsden Water. From the Post office head away from Todmorden on the roadside footway: parallel Square Road gives a break from the main road. Back on the main road it bridges the railway and passes an extensive garden centre and a cricket club. Leave shortly after the Border Rose pub by turning up an enclosed path on the near side of the Waggon & Horses. At the top, Allescholes farm road is met: across, a thin path rises steeply left, climbing above a waterfall in a wooded clough, then up wooden steps to rejoin the road on easier gradients. Go left, rising steadily to pass the Allescholes farms, then levelling out to end beneath Moor Hey Farm. Advance along the unsurfaced continuation to a gate beneath a small wood onto reedy rough pasture.

A firm level track heads away, rapidly passing Allescholes milestone at a branch path. Impressively perched just beneath the path, it bears the distances to Todmorden, Rochdale, Burnley and Halifax. Your outward route traces this historic packhorse way of Reddyshore Scout Gate high above the Summit railway tunnel, with excellent views over the Walsden Gorge backed by Blackstone Edge. The track suddenly finds itself above a craggy drop, with an air-shaft by your return route below. A gate between pylons sees the way becomes enclosed, but quickly runs even more dramatically atop the crest of Reddyshore Scout, whose steep crags add a dramatic foreground to the views. The now steadily descending rough road shortly merges into Reddyshore Farm drive to drop between air-shafts onto an abandoned road.

Double back left down the road as far as an air-shaft by lively Owler Clough. This marks the county boundary, confirmed by an old boundary stone by the wall on the right. Briefly glimpsed on the road junction below is the hexagonal Steanor Bottom Toll House. At the boundary, take a super green path rising gently left to head back towards Reddyshore Scout. This one however will run beneath the cliffs, parallel with your outward leg. Rising to a gate/stile beneath a steep crag, it rises further to ease out beneath further crags. A level stroll leads to a stile below a pylon, where you cross a streamlet to an air-shaft. Here the path begins a steady descent through bracken to another shaft, just past which it meets a broader path descending from the old milestone. This angles down the last section and past a final shaft to a gate onto a drive. Across, go down a snicket to another drive joining the main road.

Cross and go briefly left to steps down to Bottomley Road, with the northern entrance to the Summit Tunnel just to the left. Advance past cottages to the Rochdale Canal at Bottomley Lock, and go left on the towpath, a splendid stride passing several locks descending into Walsden. At Travis Mill Lock you join a road alongside tall-spired St Peter's church, turning left to finish.

The Rochdale Canal from Reddyshore Scout

27 Gorpley Clough

4 miles from Gauxholme

Varied moorland paths and a splendid wooded clough

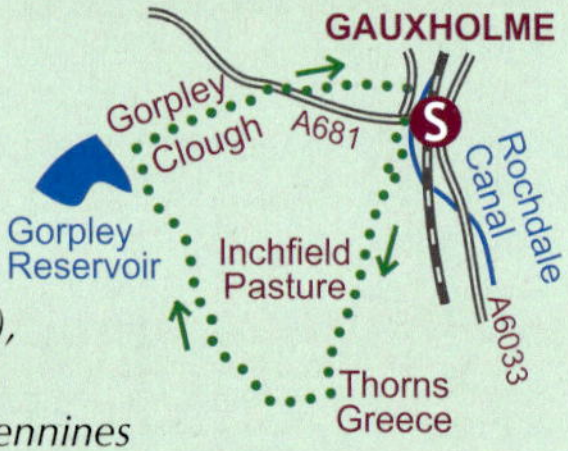

Start *Rail viaduct at A681 junction (SD 930231; OL14 7PN), roadside parking on Bacup road*
Map *OS Explorer OL21, South Pennines*

A mile south of Todmorden, Gauxholme's long, low railway viaduct overlooks the Masons Arms. From the main road pass under the viaduct, past the pub and over the Rochdale Canal. With tall gritstone crags on the right, turn left on short-lived Naze Road. From a gate on the left by modern housing, a short track rises to a gate. Immediately doubling back, a steep climb of The Naze ensues on a well engineered zigzag. This next mile traces a packhorse route from Todmorden towards Rochdale. Look back over the map-like view of the valley floor with railway, road, canal and mills. Above a bridle-gate a part setted sunken section winds up between low ruins, where ignore a branch left. Continuing up, a short walled section leads to a gate onto open moor. Joining a firm track just ahead, go briefly left. As it bears left at a wall corner take the lesser fork straight ahead, a stone causeway gently rising arrow-like across Inchfield Pasture. At a stream crossing the path deteriorates, but keep right at a fork a little further to join broad, unsurfaced Foul Clough Road just above Thorns Greece Farm.

Turn right, rising to a minor brow with two houses to the left, then slanting gently right into a minor clough. Here a slender path is signed right onto rough moorland, rising gently with regular marker posts. A line of pylons by the steeper slopes of Oatley Hill to the left might tempt you onto drier slopes as a less savoury quarter-mile on the brow involves negotiating swampy reeds. The terrain improves on a steady descent revealing Gorpley Reservoir in a fold of the hills. More steeply it drops to the base of the final pylon in front of wooded Gorpley Clough, then a green track runs the final paces left to a gate in a wall. Bridging an outflow from the reservoir, it drops right on an enclosed course along the base of the grassy dam to a treatment plant. Alongside it a small gate on the right sends a part stepped path slanting into Gorpley Clough, a charming wooded dell whose tinkling stream's enchanting moments include two lovely waterfalls. This same path leads unerringly down, crossing and re-crossing to ultimately emerge onto the Bacup road at a parking area.

Turn briefly right on the footway past an old mill, then escape at a gap on the left beyond a house. From a stile just above, a splendid path rises through Stones Wood, leaving by a kissing-gate after a small clough. The path crosses two fields to a junction of old green ways in front of a derelict old house: rise left between walls, and through the gate/stile at the top keep right across a field bottom. From a stile at the end, cross unkempt ground past a stable block at Watty Farm to use a fence-stile onto the access road. Go right to the end of the house, and just in front is a wall-stile with a very steep drop onto a green way. A few strides to the left this meets a steep path perched dramatically above the valley, with an amazing bird's-eye view. Turn right down the broadening path to finish, emerging onto Pexwood Road just short of the main road.

In Gorpley Clough

28 SALTER RAKE

4¼ miles from Todmorden

Sustained interest from moortop to towpath: easily traced paths include a classic length of packhorse route

Start *Town centre (SD 936241; OL14 5AA), car parks*
Map *OS Explorer OL21, South Pennines*

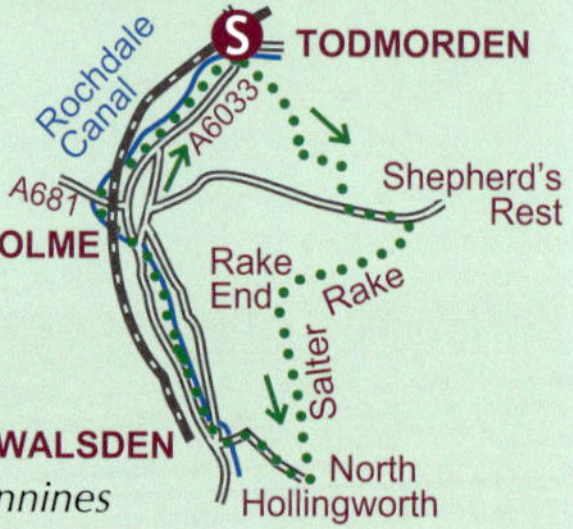

From the central roundabout outside the imposing Town Hall of 1875, head south on the Rochdale road the short way to the Golden Lion at Fielden Square, bridging the Rochdale Canal en route. Cross the side road to Honey Hole Road: rising steeply away, it jinks beneath the tall-spired Unitarian Church, climbs past the clustered houses of Honey Hole, and then a sharp kink takes it above the rear of the churchyard. With a grassy centre it pulls steeply above a wooded clough to some cottages. The unsurfaced continuation bears left, more gently now between walls. On your right is a 17th century Quaker burial ground, while ahead is the moorland skyline of Langfield Common. The lane swings sharp left to a junction by Longfield equestrian centre, with Stoodley Pike monument high ahead. Keep right, rising onto the Lumbutts road.

Go left on a short, gentle rise to the Shepherd's Rest pub. Immediately opposite, a gate onto the moorland of Langfield Common sends a grassy track rising gently way. Within a minute you meet the causeway of Salter Rake, part of a packhorse route bringing salt from Cheshire. Turn right on it, rising to a gate off the moor. A walled way rises past an inscribed guidestone to soon re-emerge onto moorland above a lone house. With massive open views over the rough moors surrounding Todmorden, the old causey resumes a superb, gently angled course, curving left at the end up onto the walk's summit at a path crossroads at Rake End.

Your way is straight on, starting a gentle slant down the moor, with stone flags returning as you look down on Walsden's steep-sided valley. This grand stride ultimately becomes enclosed at North Hollingworth. Joining a driveway at this little hamlet, advance briefly to a junction, and turn right on the surfaced access road's steep descent to the valley. At the bottom is the brief option of a setted short-cut as the road doubles back down to the edge of Walsden. A house on the right was the residence of Nobel prize-winning scientist Sir John Cockcroft. Passing tall-spired St Peter's church you meet the Rochdale Canal at Travis Mill Lock. Across it turn right on the towpath, all the way back into Todmorden.

Interest along the way includes a number of locks, and also the stream of Walsden Water running parallel for a lengthy spell: a fish-shop is also handily placed. The only break comes when the main road intervenes: you must rise to cross both it and the canal to resume on the opposite bank. Approaching the Bacup road you pass under a rail bridge alongside the Gauxholme Arches, with the Masons Arms to the right. Under the Bacup road the railway soon crosses back above, and nearer the end features an enormous brick retaining wall. Here you curve round to rejoin the road on which you began alongside Library Lock, whose vertical bottom gate permits boats' access beneath the road.

Rochdale Canal, Walsden

29 BRIDE STONES

4½ miles from Lydgate

Outstanding rock formations and old causeys on steep slopes

Start *Post office (SD 923255; OL14 8EX), 1½ miles north-west of Todmorden on A646, parking on Church Road*

Map *OS Explorer OL21, South Pennines*

Access *Open Access, see page 4*

Leave the main road by Church Road at the Post office/shop, and at the end go right on Owlers Walk. An enclosed path passes right of the last house to emerge at an immense railway arch. Pass beneath it on an access road, then a small gate on the right sends steps climbing to a stile. Resume up a fieldside, and when the fence goes left continue up a distinct hollow to Rake Farm. Go right of the houses onto the drive, then pass behind them to a gate. A path heads away above the garden, rising to an intriguing corner stile. Don't use it, but remain on the path slanting right to a small gate into a walled way. This climbs then runs left to another bend in front of the open country of Stannally Stones.

Don't enter, but climb to emerge onto a drive at Rake Hey. Passing left of the house, another walled way curves up to the old packhorse track of Stony Lane. Turn right for a grand stride with big Calderdale views. Emerging onto a reedy pasture, an unbroken causey crosses to a gate onto Whirlaw Common. Take the right-hand flagged path heading away: curving beneath Whirlaw Stones it remains flagged until becoming enclosed. A little further, above East Whirlaw Farm, double back left up a wallside track. This swings right above the wall and climbs further, closing in on the wall again to a gate/stile at the top corner by a carved gatepost.

Ascend the steep road past Windy Harbour Farm. On easing out at Mast Farm continue on, but at a gentle brow make use of Open Access and take a stile on the left. A thin trod bears gently right to a stile at a fence/wall corner, then resumes left with the fence on Bride Stones Moor. Level with the first boulders above, leave the little path to rise the short way to them. The Great Bride Stones are an extensive group of rocks, the first ones including a detached gem. Advance along the crest to the OS column at 1437ft/438m, then resume (the main path is set a little back from the edge). The path declines gently with further lower outcrops below, and heads on through two faint old walls. You soon arrive at a further cluster in line with Coal Clough windfarm, immediately above two houses on a plantation edge at Orchan House Farm.

A broader green path resumes, dropping slightly to a gate off the moor. Joining an access track at the wood edge, drop left down it to Orchan House. Pass between the houses out into a field below those final rocks. Here take a grass track right down the field centre to a gate, and down rougher pasture to a gateway onto a junction at Stony Lane. From a bridle-gate/stile in front, a path bears right across heathery Hudson Moor to drop to Hudson Bridge. Don't cross, but take the path doubling back left, steadily down with Orchan Rocks just visible to the left. At a wall at the bottom, go left a few strides to a gate. A grassy fenceside track drops below a heathery bank, meeting a broad path from the left. Through a gate/stile at the bottom corner you join an access road from the left. Turn down its enclosed course, absorbing a farm drive for a lengthy drop through Kitson Wood. Reaching civilisation turn left after the first house on Church Hill access road, dropping onto Church Road.

The Bride Stones

30 Blake Dean

4 miles from Widdop

Easy walking above lovely streams in colourful country

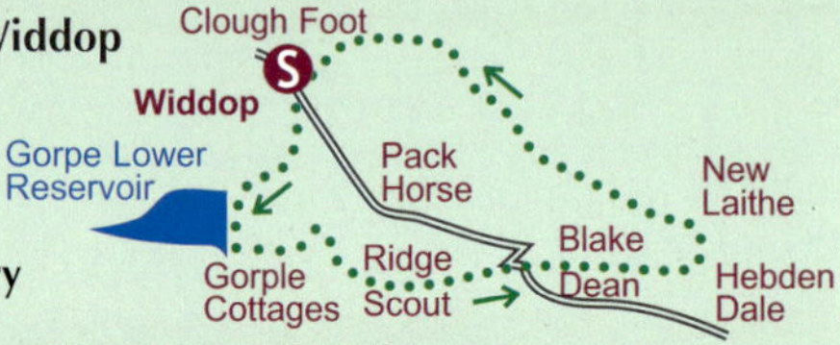

Start *Clough Foot (SD 947323; HX7 7AT), parking area half-mile west of Pack Horse Inn*
Map *OS Explorer OL21, South Pennines*

Cross the road to an access road rising to Gorple Lower Reservoir, and across the dam keep left to Gorple Cottages. Just past them take a path dropping left, soon becoming a stone causey. At the bottom, cross twin footbridges at a charming watersmeet beneath a crag in Graining Water's narrow valley. Across, take the path upstream to a small gate, where another causey slants up to a level path along the valley rim. Go right on it with an old wall and fence, which later depart. The path maintains a delightful level course through Ridge Scout's scattered rocks and bracken, and as more imposing outcrops appear, it descends gently into denser bracken (claustrophobic in high summer). Down beneath the largest outcrops is a gate, with a stile onto a road just beyond. The building in front looks over a Baptist Chapel burial ground.

Turn downhill, taking a gateway on the left between a drive and Blake Dean Bridge. A path descends steps and along the short way to a footbridge on Alcomden Water in Blake Dean. This colourful watersmeet has grassy banks and green islands beneath steep slopes. Take the main path climbing away, crossing an old railway cutting and across grassy moor to a small fence-gate. A path heads off along the top of a wooded bank to emerge into an open area: from a small gate in the adjacent wall, ascend two fieldsides onto an access road at New Laithe. Turn left for a long, level stride, ultimately dropping to Alcomden Water at Holme Ends. Across the bridge ascend to an open area, where fork left to join Walshaw Dean water company road. Go left to finish, and a bridle-gate on the left just before the road cuts a tiny corner.